# JEWHER ILHAM

## A UYGHUR'S FIGHT
## TO FREE HER FATHER

Adam Braver and Ashley Barton

*Jewher Ilham:*
*A Uyghur's Fight to Free Her Father*

ISBN: 978-1-60801-105-6

eISBN: 978-1-60801-120-9

Cover and Book Design by Alex Dimeff

Photos courtesy of Jewher Ilham unless otherwise noted.

Library of Congress Cataloging-in-Publication Data

Ilham, Jewher.
  Jewher Ilham : a Uyghur daughter's fight to free her father
/ edited by Adam Braver and Ashley Barton ; interviews
conducted by Adam Braver, Ashley Barton, and Molly
Gessford.
      pages cm -- (Broken silence series)
   ISBN 978-1-60801-105-6
1. Ilham, Jewher--Interviews. 2. Uighur (Turkic people)--
Interviews. 3. Ilham, Jewher--Family. 4. Fathers and daughters-
-China. 5. Tohti, Ilham, 1969- 6. Political activists--China-
-Biography. 7. Human rights workers--China--Biography.
8. Political prisoners--China--Biography. 9. Uighur (Turkic
people)--China--Biography. 10. Uighur (Turkic people)--Civil
rights--China. I. Braver, Adam, 1963- II. Barton, Ashley. III.
Gessford, Molly. IV. Title.
  DS731.U4I54 2015
  362.82'95092--dc23
  [B]

**UNO PRESS**
unopress.org

# JEWHER ILHAM

## A UYGHUR'S FIGHT TO FREE HER FATHER

INTERVIEWED AND EDITED BY ADAM BRAVER AND ASHLEY BARTON
FOREWORD BY U.S. SENATOR SHERROD BROWN
AFTERWORD BY ROBERT QUINN

**UNO PRESS**

*Photo: Echo Lu*

# FOREWORD
## U.S. SENATOR SHERROD BROWN
## WASHINGTON, D.C.

AT THE AGE OF 18, Jewher Ilham stood in line to board a plane to the United States with her father for a quick trip to Indiana University. She stood with businessmen and students, expecting a short stay in Bloomington, where she would help her father, Ilham Tohti, settle into the town where he would spend a year as a visiting professor.

Ilham Tohti would never board that plane—but his daughter would, and thus would begin her transformation from teenager to human rights activist.

Her father was detained at the Beijing airport by Chinese authorities, beaten and interrogated, but Jewher was given a gut-wrenching choice: she could return to her life in China with her father, where their family faced persecution as a result of her father's advocacy for the Uyghur ethnic minority group, or travel on to the United States, alone, with no plan for the future.

Jewher got on that airplane that day, and in a new, strange country she would carry on her father's efforts to promote peaceful dialogue and an understanding of the plight of her people, the Uyghurs. Before her 20th birthday, Jewher was taking on one of the world's largest and most oppressive governments.

Under President Xi Jinping, Chinese officials have detained hundreds of peaceful advocates for reform. Among the hardest hit have been Jewher and her father's Uyghur people. For decades, they have suffered religious and cultural repression that has exacerbated ethnic tensions. Ilham Tohti was one of the most prominent and eloquent voices to speak out. In most societies, citizens like him, who sought to foster a dialogue between Uyghurs and the majority Han population, would be celebrated. But in China, they go to jail.

It was Jewher's bravery advocating for her father's cause that led us to cross paths in the spring of 2014, when she testified at a hearing before the Congressional-Executive Commission on China.

If Jewher was nervous when she spoke, it did not show. Leaning into the microphone to address Members of Congress, she spoke eloquently about what it was like for her family to live in a police state. In measured tones, she described the constant harassment and surveillance they faced as a result of her father's advocacy: coming home from school to find an empty house because the family had been sent away; authorities ramming her father's car; the government threatening to kill her family, including her two very young brothers.

When Jewher and her father said goodbye at the airport, he told her to be strong; she didn't know when she would ever see him again. And in January of 2014, dozens of Chinese police officers again came to Ilham Tohti's house, and took him away, this time for good. Jewher and her family have not been able to see or talk to him since, yet Jewher continues to fight his fight, which has become her fight. She tells his story, which is the story of so many nameless, faceless activists in China whose voices have been silenced.

Jewher has shown a courage and conviction few of us could imagine. She has pulled the curtain on the human toll of China's oppression, and shown the world that in China it is not only the advocates who suffer, but whole families. Children are unable to register for school. Jobs and livelihoods are threatened. Daughters are separated from their fathers.

Jewher's story is the untold story of China and the Uyghur people, the one that the Chinese government does not want us to hear, and one that fewer and fewer are able to tell. That's why it is so important that Jewher has spoken out, and why we must make sure she is not forgotten. This book is proof that Jewher and her people will not be silenced.

# INTRODUCTION
## ADAM BRAVER,
### BROKEN SILENCE SERIES EDITOR

I THINK IT WAS a phone call. Maybe it was an email. Regardless, I had just let Elliot Sperling know that Jewher Ilham had arrived safely in Washington, D.C. A little confusion had stemmed from being in two different terminals, but after comparing landmarks via cell phone calls, my two students (one being Ashley Barton, who is coediting this book), Jewher, and I finally found each other in Terminal B at National Airport. Since Jewher had ended up in Bloomington, Indiana the prior year at age eighteen, Elliot had become her de facto caretaker, her true confidant, the one entrusted with her well-being and future, commissioned by fate to be the right person who was there at the exact right time. Elliot's reply to me: "Please take good care of her."

I hadn't before met Jewher. We only had spoken by phone and through messaging. Along with some students, I had arranged several meetings for and with her in D.C. It took some convincing on our part. Jewher was cautious. There were people and organizations that she worried might be trying to use her for their own purposes. She didn't want to take any steps that she perceived as possibly incurring further harm on her father in China. Plus, she didn't even know who we were. But ultimately, learning that we had no greater agenda other than our commitment to protecting freedom of expression; that on our end there were undergraduates her age primarily involved; and that through a collaboration we represented the NGO Scholars at Risk, Jewher finally accepted our invitation to meet in D.C.

"I think this is a good thing," I remember her telling me.

After months of relative silence on the state of her father (for very good reason), she was ready to do something. She trusted us.

Our Washington itinerary would have Jewher telling the story of her father in offices from Foggy Bottom to Capitol Hill. It was similar to work my students and I had done in the past with Scholars at Risk and PEN American Center. We felt practiced. Readied. But would Jewher?

At the time, we didn't know that we would find ourselves at such a climactic moment of Jewher's new storyline. The moment where she would find the confidence in her voice to speak out on behalf of her father. Or, perhaps, even feel ready to shout out to the world about the injustice of his situation.

I honored Elliot's words to take care of her. We accompanied Jewher to more than a half-dozen meetings in one day. With each new conference, we heard her take more and more control over the room. By the end of all of our visits, she had a date set to testify before the Congressional-Executive Committee on China. She had a promise from a member of the China desk at State to take up the issue of her little brothers being under constant surveillance. And Senators Jack Reed and Sheldon Whitehouse would co-write a letter to the Chinese Ambassador on behalf of her father.

She also gained a new set of friends—my two students, both young women, her age. (And I hope, if it is not too presumptuous, I can include myself as one Jewher's friends, despite not being anywhere near her age.) We acted like intimates, not like strangers who, just the night before, cell phones glued to ears, had been trying to find each other in the airport terminals. In a matter of twenty-four hours we were bouncing from conversations about the frightening experiences she had endured under China's regime, to searching for ice cream, to looking at pictures of her friends and her cooking on her iPhone, to having Jewher order for us at a Korean restaurant—in Korean!

Hers may have been a life burdened by her circumstance, but it was one that also loosed a free spirit when it felt like overtaking her. In her, we saw hope, gravity, levity, and stubborn confidence all rolled into one.

Still, that does not preclude the experience she's had, or the calling that was brought upon her, or the uncertainty that the days ahead will bring. Nor is it to suggest that she doesn't worry. Doesn't doubt herself. Or doesn't question her circumstances. Doesn't everyone at twenty? But how many of you saw your father taken away from you, and thirty-six hours later found yourself in a foreign country, without the language, with the wrong visa, and with little understanding of where you just were, and where you were going?

To GIVE SOME LARGER context, the Uyghur people are among fifty-six recognized ethnic minorities in the People's Republic of China. They are of Turkic descent, and in China, they are most synonymous with the Xinjiang region in Western China. When they settled in the region is debatable. Many Uyghur people will say that they are indigenous peoples to Xinjiang. Chinese historians track their arrival to the ninth century. Regardless, there are centuries of tensions between the Uyghur people and the dominant Han Chinese. Modern history has seen the strains demonstrated through several events, most notably the now notorious Urumqi riots in July 2009, where demonstrations by Uyghur for "self-determination" turned to protests that ended up in violent clashes that led to a reported 200 deaths and scores more injuries. To the Han Chinese, the aftermath fermented the idea of Uyghur people as violent and dangerous. It led to tighter restrictions. And, as so often happens when people feel oppressed, resentments are built, and from those resentments come some people who feel more radicalized, and a subset of that group may bring the idea of using violence against the dominant regime. There is talk of separating from the dominant regime. And a longstanding rumble only seems to get louder and more tumultuous.

But then there are people such as Ilham Tohti. Of Uyghur descent, Ilham was born in Artush, in the Xinjiang region. He came to Beijing as a graduate student to study economics, where he eventually settled into a professorship at Minzu University. In 2006 he founded a website called *Uyghur Online*. While the site was often critical of Chinese policy toward the Uyghur people in Xinjiang, the intent always focused on forging solutions for a peaceful and respectful coexistence. It is in this context that Ilham became known as a "moderate voice."

Maybe it was because the site had readership in and out of China?

Maybe it was a result of heightened fears following the Urumqi riots?

Soon Ilham caught the attention of the Chinese authorities—this moderate voice now became portrayed as someone who was inciting violence, and even worse, advocating separatism. Several times he was detained. Placed under house arrest. Threatened. And yet he persevered with his work on *Uyghur Online*, still envisioning a Xinjiang in which Han Chinese and Uyghur people could co-exist beyond the inherent and historical tensions.

In 2013, he agreed to come to Indiana University for one year as a visiting scholar. He planned to bring his eighteen year old, Beijing-born daughter, Jewher, with him. She would stay for just one month during her winter school break. But as they prepared to board the plane, Ilham suddenly was detained, and in the mayhem, Jewher ended up alone on the U.S.-bound flight, after her father, while in police custody at the airport, implored her to go to the U.S. and to never come back.

One year later, after a continuing pattern of threats and house arrests, Ilham was arrested and detained, and almost eight months later was formally charged for separatism—a charge that could bring the death penalty at its worst, and a life sentence at its best.

And lest readers of this book wonder if indeed Ilham was a separatist who was inciting violence though his website *Uyghur Online*, I direct you to the following comments:

> —*Secretary of State John Kerry.* "Ilham Tohti is known to the world for his many years working to foster mutual understanding, tolerance, and dialogue to peacefully promote harmony and unity between Uighurs and Han Chinese. His detention silenced an important moderate Uighur voice. Mr. Tohti and those like him are indispensable in helping to resolve the underlying causes of unrest and violence. Silencing them can only make tensions worse."

> —*The White House.* "He is a respected professor who has long championed efforts to bridge differences between Uighurs and Han Chinese. We believe that civil society leaders like Ilham Tohti play a vital role in reducing the sources of inter-ethnic tension in China, and should not be persecuted for peacefully expressing their views."

> —*The European Union.* "The EU condemns the life sentence for alleged "separatism" handed out today to Uighur economics professor Ilham Tohti, which is completely unjustified."

WHEN ASHLEY, MOLLY GESSFORD, and I met with Jewher in Bloomington, Indiana to begin this book, it was the weekend before her father's trial would begin in Xinjiang. The weekend of September 13, 2014, to be exact. She hadn't seen him since that fateful night at the airport. And though they had Skyped for much of 2013, it had been nearly eight months since she'd had any contact with him.

Already there were many questions being raised about the fairness of the trial. For example, why was it being held in the high-tension region of Xinjiang when the alleged crime was committed nearly 1,500 miles away in Beijing? Why was Ilham's lawyer denied access to certain pieces of evidence? Were the proceedings really being closed because of state secrets? To many international observers, there was a sense that this only would be a show trial. That the Chinese Authority's belief already had been cemented that Ilham Tohti had, as the New York Times reported, "'bewitched and coerced young ethnic students' into working on his website and that he had 'built a criminal syndicate' . . . and 'internationalized' the Uighur issue by giving interviews to foreign reporters and had translated foreign articles and essays about Xinjiang to be posted on *Uighur Online*."

Although hope was the dominant emotion of the weekend, fear and anticipation of the expected result of next week's trial across the globe was the undercurrent to any positive rationalization. By this point, no matter how many protests were raised by officials around the world, the Chinese authorities had dug in on this case. Needless to say, despite a long weekend that included a lot of laughter, gastronomic pleasures, and plenty of conversation, one could not help but be aware that a new and darker chapter potentially was about to be introduced to this story.

Over the course of the weekend (and much is contained within the subsequent pages) we learned the story of a young first-year college student (very much still a little girl, by her own admission) who had to grow up and reshape her life. Previously, she never had lived alone or had to fend for herself. She'd had little interest in politics (and in fact, for her own well being, was discouraged by her father to become involved in his issues). But now she found herself in a foreign land, in the middle of an international incident, with only the remarkable Elliot Sperling as a guide.

We heard about the concerns. The bureaucratic machinations. The belief it all would be temporary. The realization when it seemed it might be more permanent (which had led to that first trip to Washington). The strength to overcome her own inner conflicts about her ability to make a difference when she testified before Congress. And how, when in front of nearly seven hundred luminaries and influencers in New York City, she brought down the house with her acceptance speech on behalf of her father for the Barbara Goldsmith Freedom to Write Award at the PEN American Center's 2014 annual gala.

But here are some of the other things we took away:

- If you are one of her guests, Jewher will cook you traditional meals such as dapanji or pilaf. In the Chinese and Middle Eastern markets of Bloomington she will parse each cut of chicken. Each shank of lamb. Inspecting them in the way that a fine craftsman evaluates all his materials. She will shoo away your efforts to pay, with a wave of the hand that easily could turn to a slap of the wrist. She will insist on buying all the ingredients.

- She will go silent when eating a banana split at the Chocolate Moose on South Walnut Street. And she will laugh at you for feeling almost sick when you finish a gigantic triple-layered chocolate Blizz that you swore was too much for you, but you kept eating anyway.

- She will not apologize for being silly. For being opinionated. Or for being loud.

- She will make extra food with every meal, and deliver it to her neighbors.

- She has a remarkable network of friends in Bloomington, with texts pinging on her phone nearly every minute.

- She will take you to one of her most personal spots just outside of Bloomington, Lake Monroe, to show you where she comes for peace and meditation when the anxieties start to rise.

- Whenever you show her a picture you've taken of her, she will make you try to delete it, saying she looks fat. (She doesn't.)

- She will say that her English is horrible. (It isn't.)

- She will tear up at the exact moment that she tells you that throughout this ordeal she has had to learn to not express her concerns as emotional.

- She will confess that despite the horrible circumstances that befell her father, and that landed her in America, that she actually feels more suited to life in the United States. That as an outspoken, opinionated young woman she never quite felt like she fit-in in China. In the U.S., she'll tell you, her personality has a kinship with American social mores, especially for women.

In other words, this is not just a person telling a series of startling events. Much as a plotline really isn't *the* story, what happened (and continues to happen) with Jewher is not who she is. Yes, the events have shaped her. Yes, they have changed the course of her life. But the temptation must be resisted to cast this narrative as one of an ordinary person who got caught in an extraordinary situation. After getting to know Jewher Ilham over the past two years, I think I can safely say that this is a narrative about an *extraordinary* person who became cast into an unexpected extraordinary situation.

PLEASE TAKE CARE OF HER.

When the three of us said goodbye to Jewher in the hotel lobby after our first meeting in Washington, D.C., I remember thinking: Take care of *her*? I think I'd feel better if Jewher were taking care of me.

# PART ONE

On February 2nd 2013, we didn't tell anybody.

We came.

We went to the airport.

*    *    *

My father always said, "Oh, a lot of universities in America would like *me* to be a professor."

"Okay," I said. "Okay." I didn't believe him. I'd thought maybe he was just saying this to impress me. He always talked like this, kind of teasing. *Your dad can sing. Your dad can draw. Your dad can blah-blah-blah.* I figured he was kidding when he started talking about teaching in America. One more thing.

On the evening of January 2nd, he asked me, "So, do you ever want to go to America again?" We were in our apartment in Beijing. My stepmother and two little brothers were out somewhere. I was getting ready for the winter break. It was my first year of college.

"Sure, of course I want to go again." I'd been there once with my dance troupe when I was fourteen.

Then he looked at me with a more serious expression. "Do you want to go with me?"

I didn't really take it as serious. My father likes to joke. Especially with me. "In the future," I replied.

But then he showed me an invitation letter from Indiana University. It read that they were inviting him as a visiting scholar. And it said that he could take one person with him for a month. A family member. And because my stepmom couldn't speak English, and my brothers were too little, he said I would be the best person. In the US, I could cook for him, and clean his apartment.

Maybe because I'd been to the US before, it didn't sound as exciting. But also it was my school break. I said that. I told him, "I want to stay with my friends. We've been making plans."

"Too bad. You're coming."

He thought I'd be super happy. *America!*

He added, "And we're leaving in February."

I didn't want to argue with him. What could I say? Even if I'd said no, I would still have to go. It was better to say okay and make him happy, even though—and I told him this—it would be kind of boring to stay with your father in an apartment for a whole month. Cooking for him every day.

That is how I thought then. I was young. But in a way, I think it's much better than what I think about now—just waiting for him to get released.

Now, I'd cook every day for him.

ON THE WAY TO the airport we were checking to see if someone was following us. It had happened many times before. For example, when my father and I would go shopping, there would be cars trailing us. Sometimes it was like in a movie, changing directions and trying to get away.

We'd bought the tickets very early in the morning, planning to leave in the middle of the night—at four AM—in order not to draw attention. I didn't sleep the whole night.

Nobody followed us. It was all good.

We went to check the baggage; it was overweight, which would require an extra charge that we didn't want to pay. So we shifted some items between our bags to change the balance. That took a long time. But finally we got the bags through, and we made our by train to the international terminal.

I stopped and took a picture.

"I thought it would be harder for us," my father said. "But we've been successful."

Because I was at boarding school, I didn't know a lot about my father's work with the Uyghur people. I was fifteen, sleeping at school not far from our apartment because my father had told me to.

Our apartment had turned into a hotel for homeless Uyghur families. It was not a large space, but it was enough for my father to house Uyghur children and parents who had taken to begging on the streets of Beijing. He would serve them food until they found a new place to live.

When I would come home on the weekends I would eat with them and learn who they were and the struggles they had gone through.

I grew to like the business of our home. It made the dinners with my family even more interesting.

My father values education very highly, and so the majority of my time away from school was spent studying in my room or at the library. I had little time to sit and just talk to my father. Still, I knew that things weren't right between my father and the government. My father began to be more involved in Uyghur issues; he saw clearly that the tensions between the Uyghur and Han Chinese were only escalating, so he created his website, *Uyghur Online*, as an open forum to ease the tension and create discourse across ethnic lines. At first the website was unfiltered; anyone could say anything, comment on any article and post any information. But my father was careful about these types of things; if extremists posted on his website, he was quick to take those posts down. His goal was not to incite violence or promote extremists' points of view; his aim was to alleviate ethnic boundaries, and that could only be done through moderate reasoning and discussion. If opinions are too extreme, it undermines the other perspectives, and that is never a good thing. My father was the token for moderate voices. But the government, they didn't see him this way.

During some weeks when I was at school, a policeman would come to visit my family's apartment as a "friend" and sit and talk with my father. Sometimes this "friend" would take my family for a short "vacation." This "vacation" was the kind where there were no phones, no computers, and no communication.

I was scared the first few times I came home to an empty apartment. No one would be there.

But after awhile, I grew used to these sporadic "travels." I was so young and naïve; I didn't understand the gravity of these visits. I believed the police were my father's friends.

I believed everything.

I knew nothing.

But in the summer of July 2009, after my second year at boarding school, I started to understand. After the riots in Urumqi, the capital city of the Xinjiang region, the government began to pay greater attention to my father. I was still young during these riots, but as I understood it, it started out as a series of protests by the

Uyghur people and quickly escalated to violence against the Han Chinese. After several days, more than one hundred and fifty Chinese people had been killed. The government suspected that my father was the one who organized the riots. But this could not be true. He was having a visit from one of his "friends" at this time; he was under house arrest.

By my third year in school, I became even more aware of my father's situation. He was always a quiet man, but during these times, he grew even quieter. I saw the sense of worry in his eyes. He looked older to me, more worn down.

The "vacations" grew longer. Sometimes my family disappeared for two weeks. Then it became three weeks.

I grew more anxious. I barely slept.

The few times I did see my father, I knew that he had slept even less; it was as if the burden of the Uyghur people fell solely on his shoulders.

The family in Beijing (2012)

THEY LED US TO a small room with a camera. Actually they took him.

"Where are you taking my father?" I pleaded, following them.

They ignored me. They wouldn't talk to me at all.

Just moments earlier, we'd been standing in line, waiting to be called to the last step before boarding—having our passports stamped.

I went first with no problem. They looked up some information on the computer, and then called me forward. It only took a second. But when I looked back, my father was waiting there, still waiting to be called.

One minute.

Two minutes.

Then it had turned to ten minutes.

When my father asked what was happening, the immigration officials would repeat, *We are checking, we are checking.*

Finally they told my father, "Please come with us."

"Why should I come with you?" he said. "I have done everything legally. I have all the documents. Why do you want me come with you? If you want to say anything, just say it here!" My father explained to them that our flight was waiting to board; that we had to go now, if we were going to make it.

I thought, *what happens if we are not able to go there?*

The immigration officer, a young man, said that if we were allowed to continue on, he'd make sure we'd still catch the flight. Don't worry. And then they began to lead my father away.

I heard him ask, "What about my luggage? . . . What about my luggage?"

When they didn't reply, he asked me about the bag.

I said, "Dad, is it really the time to think about that?"

"They're not going to let me go right now," he said. "You go ahead." It was just a temporary hold up; he just didn't want his baggage left behind.

I ended up with his suitcase. I hadn't realized it would be so heavy.

I still have it. His shoes. His jackets. His sweaters. They all are with me.

Every time somebody asks, *Who did you come to America with?* I say, it was *supposed* to be my father. They say, *Is he coming?*

I think so, I tell them. I have his suitcase waiting.

And I followed them. That's how we'd ended up in the room.

I was so scared! My father was such a strict man. Nobody argued with him. Never ever. But now I was seeing someone pulling my father so roughly.

"Why are you talking to my father? Why are you doing this to him?"

I was so freaked out.

So angry.

And so afraid.

My father looked at me. "Don't cry," he commanded. He saw my tears welling. They could fall at any moment. "Don't cry."

Because I never faced this kind of situation before, I was scared I would forget everything. If they are mistreating my father, I thought, I have to have evidence. So I turned on my phone. And I began to record.

It was a very small room with no windows, like the size of a bathroom. There was one camera. Two chairs without backs. And one guy who kept watch, sitting with us, making sure I would not run away.

"Why you are doing this to me?" my father said to the guard. "I have everything authorized."

"We only are following the legal steps."

My father looked like he could burst. "I *have* the full legal steps. Why don't you let me go?"

"We are checking. We are checking."

We sat there for two hours in that little room in the Beijing airport, listening to the immigration officers repeat *we are checking, we are checking.*

All I could think is: What is going on? How are they going to treat us? Are we going to jail?

We only had to get on the plane. Then we could go to Indiana. It should have been so simple.

We didn't do anything wrong.

I was so confused. My mind went very messy.

PICTURE US IN JEWHER'S apartment in Bloomington, Indiana. The complex, a few miles from the Indiana University campus, is a fairly large assemblage of units that look as though it dates back a couple of decades, part and parcel of typical student housing. Jewher tells us many of the residents are international students. Walk upstairs into her apartment, and you'll enter into the living room. Off to the left is a dining area, adjacent to a kitchen that extends back and out of sight of the common area. Straight to the back are two bedrooms. From one of them wafts harp music; Jewher's roommate is a graduate student in music. Baroque melodies coming from the gentle strings will be an ongoing soundtrack for much of the weekend. Also in the bedroom is a little white dog, a Pomeranian called Arya. She is happy and excitable. She only comes out for supervised visits. We will spend much of the time in the living room. It is sparsely appointed, but doesn't feel empty. On a table against the wall, where you'd expect a TV, there are tchotchkes of some of Jewher's favorite cartoon characters placed among family photographs taken in China. A friend has made a sketch of her father, which in its simple black and white pencil strokes has a way of making him seem present in the room. While much of the formal interviewing will take place on the couch in the living room or at the dining room table, most of the social time centers in the kitchen.

*Editors*: And so it's what? It's carrots—

*Jewher*: Carrots, onions, lamb, rice, I put tomatoes on it, because it makes the color good.

*Editors*: You were saying how the pilaf is what you give to people when they come and visit.

*Jewher*: It's a means of respect. Uyghur people love inviting people into their homes. How can I say? They are very friendly.

*Editors*: What makes a good pilaf? What makes a good Uyghur pilaf?

**Jewher**: When you steam the lamb with the rice, the lamb makes the rice taste of lamb. The oils from the lamb get mixed with the rice. But, I don't really know; I'm not considered as a good pilaf maker. You know I didn't like pilaf when I was younger. But my stepmother is so good at cooking pilaf that she made me love it. It became my favorite food. Before that it was lahman, which is the most popular and most common homemade Uyghur food. For that dish, we fry vegetables and then put them on top of noodles. Handmade noodles.

*Editors*: Your pilaf smells wonderful.

**Jewher**: We are supposed to eat it with our hands. A lot of elder people still eat pilaf that way. But young people feel shy and they use silverware now . . . I hope it will be delicious, because sometimes it's not always delicious.

*Editors*: Can we pick up the story now? At the airport. About how you...?

**Jewher**: [water running] Sorry, I can't hear you.

A WOMAN CAME INTO to the office where we were sitting and waiting. Looking at me, she asked: "Do you want get on the plane, or not? The flight is going to leave now." She was a pretty young woman. Actually I'm sure she didn't know anything, too; she was just doing what she was told.

I didn't say anything. I didn't know what to say.

"How can she leave by herself?" my father said. "She's my daughter. She has to go with me."

That woman ignored my father. She just stared at me. "Do you want to go or not?"

My father said, "I told you, she is a young little girl. She's only eighteen."

"Do you want to go or not?" She asked it several more times. (I have the recording for this.)

"According to her visa," my father tried to explain, "she has to go with me. If I don't go, she won't go."

"Do you want to go or not?"

My father shook his head. In that gesture, I could see both his frustration and his anger. He called me closer to him. I scooted the chair over. In a quieter voice, he asked, "Do you want to go or not?"

"Me?" I didn't expect that he would ask this question. "If you are not going, why am I going there? I was only going because of you. Why would I go there myself?"

"Get out of this place. Please, Jewher. Just go. Do you still want to stay here, since they treat us like this? Just go."

I was shocked. I started to cry.

My father suddenly got very angry. "Don't cry in front of others!" he ordered. "Don't let anybody see you cry anymore. Especially them. They will think that Uyghur girls are weak. Show them that you are strong."

I tried to hold back my tears. I was just eighteen. Here in America, everybody thinks you are an adult at that age, but in China eighteen is more like fifteen here. I could see his mind was made up. I didn't want to go, but I've said before, I can't say no to my dad. I whispered: "I don't understand. Why am I going to America by myself?"

"They treat you like this, and you still want to stay here? Go. Go."

"Do you want to get on the plane or not?"

"Yes," I said. That was the first time that I talked. It really was a bureaucratic mistake to set me on the plane. They were trying to have my father make me stay; thinking if I remained China, he would not try to go to America. I think these officials were acting by themselves; that they didn't ask the top, higher-level people. If the bosses had known it, they wouldn't have let me go. And today I think they are regretting it. I have made so much trouble for them now.

"Go. Go. Go," my father repeated, as he patted my back. And then we hugged. And then I just left. The woman took me to the flight.

ELLIOT SPERLING IS THE best person in Bloomington. He is a professor of East Asian studies at IU. And from the start, he has been involved in everything that has happened to me. I can't imagine how things would have turned out without him.

My father had met Elliot through mutual friends. Quickly, they became friends. When my father received the invitation to Indiana University, he called up Elliot. Elliot then helped us arrange our trip. He helped us find an apartment. And he agreed to pick us up at the airport.

Dear Elliot, I always tell him thank you so much for what you have done for my family. Thank you so much for what you have taught me. And thank you so much for confronting all the problems with me! I will try to be a strong person, just like you.

My teacher. My uncle. My friend.

With Elliot Sperling

MAYBE JUST TEN MINUTES or so until take off?

The woman and I were running because the flight was going to leave soon. They were calling my name over the loudspeaker. It was like a movie. *Passengers Jewher Ilham and Ilham Tohti. Passengers Jewher Ilham and Ilham Tohti.* I thought, first you guys are detaining us, and then you are announcing it as though it is my fault? It felt ridiculous. And even though there was only about ten minutes left, and even though my father was still being held, I still tried to believe he would end up on the flight with me.

But when I got on the plane, the seat beside me was empty. You can't imagine that feeling.

*Elliot Sperling*

JUST BEFORE I WENT to bed, I got a message from a friend saying that Ilham had been detained at the airport. I had these two friends who were staying with me at the time, and they heard me when I said, *Oh, fuck.* But it was late. I mean really late. So I just went to bed.

I got up in the morning to another message: *Ilham's daughter is on her way to the United States. They allowed her to get on a plane.*

Now the problem is that it's a weekend. Fortunately I had the phone numbers of people at State. Some personal numbers that I could call. I had been speaking to them already, having had some conversations about Ilham's visa, as well as Jewher's (after Ilham had asked, Can my daughter come with me)? In short, I knew where to go and I knew who was who. I immediately got on the phone.

The first issue was that Jewher was coming on a J-2 visa, which did not allow entry into the country without the J-1 visa holder, who in this case was Ilham. And the people who were doing customs and border protection in Chicago didn't know anything about Ilham Tohti. They didn't know anything about what had happened fourteen hours earlier in Beijing. They just understood: *visa, ID.* For all they knew, Jewher was illegal or was being trafficked. God knows what.

I'd had no contact with Jewher at all during this period. We were figuring all of this out while she was still in the air.

ON THE PLANE, FOR the first time, all of the Han Chinese suddenly looked so ugly to me. I'd grown up with them. Many were my friends.  But now their faces looked so—not ugly . . . Mean. They looked mean to me. Why were they doing this to us? Just because we are Uyghur?

As I was crying, I was looking at one Han Chinese woman on my right side. The left seat was empty; it was supposed be my father's. I can only imagine what my crying face looked like. "What happened?" she asked.

I couldn't even make a sound; I was crying so deep. I'm sure the whole place was looking at me.

She asked me if I was okay.

I gathered enough breath, and I told her what was going on. She just listened.

I said, "I don't have a phone. I don't have money. I don't have anything." All I had was a card with Elliot's name and number. "Can I use your phone later, because I don't know what to do?"

She was pretty nice, and said yes.

Later, when we were getting close to America, I asked her if she could help me fill out the form. I told her I don't know English.

She helped me. And I did see kindness in her. It calmed me a little bit. And then the pilot announced to prepare for landing in Chicago.

I WAITED IN THE immigration office at the airport in Chicago. Because my father wasn't with me, they wouldn't let me into the US. You see, the J-2 visa holder can only enter with the J-1 holder. I thought: *Uh, are you kidding me? I don't sleep for 40 hours or something, I don't eat the whole day because they didn't give me halal food on the plane, and are you going to do this to me?*

"Please," I said. "I don't speak English, how do I understand you? I just speak very little." I wanted to explain. "My father . . . Please . . . Detain." But they just thought it was something more. And I thought they just don't want me getting into America.

One of them asked, "Do you know anybody in America?"

"Anybody? . . . No. Oh! Oh! . . . I was supposed to be with my father . . ." I didn't really have English at that time. I was doing my best to explain, while looking for Elliot's information that my father had given me. "Arrested by police. . . My father arrested by police." When I said that, their attitude changed. It suddenly worried them about who I might be, and what was going on.

"Name card," I said, handing them Elliot's name and number. "This, this person!"

They said they'd call.

I noticed the clock. Already, I'd been there for three hours. Wasn't I supposed to be on my to Indianapolis by now? "My flight!" I said. "Flight! Go away! Go away!" I remember what I said, so full of grammar mistakes. I kept trying. "It's already go away. Go away!"

"Don't worry ma'am. Don't worry. Just, wait here."

And so I waited. Just waited. I watched the people who arrived later than me get all their documents and go to their flight. I wondered, what has happened to me? Why are they going to set me in the jail? All I could think was that I wanted to call my dad. I didn't know what to do. Even my phone wouldn't work.

From the name card they phoned Elliot. And then he called the people from the State Department. And I waited and waited until they talked to the immigration office.

*Elliot Sperling*

STATE FINALLY LEARNED SHE was being held in Chicago. "Okay," I said, "so we have to get her out of detention in Chicago."

The problem had to do with lines of control, as it were, within the bureaucracy. Customs and Border Protection doesn't answer to State; they are under Homeland Security. So during this period while Jewher was being detained in Chicago, people in Washington were calling each other to work this out.

After a while, I get the word that they were releasing her. I was on the cell phone at the Indianapolis airport because I'd already gone up to meet the flight that she was originally supposed to be on. The person on the other end told me Jewher would be *paroled* into the country. That I didn't need to worry. Customs and Border Protection in Chicago was going to escort her to the plane to Indianapolis. "Okay," I said. "Okay." But *parole* is a bureaucratic term; in other words, it meant the issue was not completely resolved. Her future status was still very much up in the air.

While I waited at the airport in Indianapolis, I actually got a text from Jewher. Her father had given her my number. I was quite surprised that she was able to call me like that. And relieved. So I texted her back, and then continued to wait.

THEN I FOUND OUT I'd be let in. Given a one-month's visa.

One day I am a very normal first year college student. The next day it is the U.S. State Department. Immigration. Police. Like a movie. It felt almost ridiculous.

A policeman took me to check my baggage. It was so cold. Freezing. Chicago that time of year. February.

I got my bags. Two *huge* bags. I still had my father's. Exhausted and hungry, I carried them with me. The policeman then handed me over to a woman. She said, "You look sick."

I said, "Hungry . . . Hungry."

"Oh, do you want to eat something?"

"Money, no . . . No money."

She said, "Poor little girl."

She bought me McDonald's. $6.25. I remember.

While I ate, she talked about her daughters. She said she had two just like me.

I didn't always understand what she was saying . . . The words sounded so fast. But what I did come to understand was that after the way people had been treating me over the past day, I suddenly saw that people in American could be nice.

I still think about her. I don't recall her face exactly, but I'll always appreciate how nice she was at the moment.

THE FLIGHT FROM CHICAGO to Indianapolis took two hours. I still couldn't sleep. And when I got off the plane, there was Elliot.

My eyes were swollen from crying so much. Plus no sleeping, and still being a little hungry. Not to mention having had *two* experiences with the police in one day: first in China, and then in America. And here I was, and I didn't even speak English.

But then Elliot spoke to me in Chinese. I was shocked. But I had no energy to react to how surprised I was that he was fluent in Chinese.

*Elliot Sperling*

FINALLY SHE CAME OUT to the passenger reception area, and I didn't know what she looked like—well I did because I had her passport photo, but she doesn't look like her passport photo—but I knew it was her because she looked absolutely shell-shocked. She told me she hadn't slept for thirty-six hours, and that the last thing she saw in China was her father being taken.

I told her I was so sorry about the situation. I said I hoped it hadn't been too bad.

She confirmed that indeed she had been escorted to the Indianapolis-bound plane; but from her description it seemed like they wanted to make sure she didn't escape into Chicago. Customs and Border Protection didn't know anything about her really, other than that she had showed up in Chicago without the proper visa she needed in order to enter the U.S. by herself. Otherwise they knew nothing about what she was doing in Chicago and seem to have assumed the worst. So they hadn't been terribly polite. I learned from Jewher that as a last step they made sure she had her seatbelt on. Buckled in. A stranger in a strange land now.

ON THE DRIVE TO Bloomington, I didn't talk about anything. I'd only answer when Elliot asked me a question. Otherwise I stared out the window. I don't really remember much. At that moment, I had no real interest of how America looked like. I was just looking.

What was I going to do now? I had no plan.

What should I do? I have nothing here.

I had no feeling. (I want to check this word in my translator. I really have to express this word. This word is very important for me.) *Numb*.

That's exactly what I felt like: Numb.

I really was so helpless.

I can't imagine any of this without Elliot. I think I would have died here.

*Elliot Sperling*

THESE TWO OLD FRIENDS of mine were staying with me at my house when Jewher arrived in the US. And I remember I jokingly said to Jewher, "Jewher, I'm so sorry, but after all of this, you now have to spend time with an old ex-hippie and his friends."

But the worst part, *the worst part*, was when she walked into my house. She's completely exhausted. And there were my two friends plus one other friend joining us for dinner. Jewher is completely dead. We open the door, and . . . *Ruff, ruff!* At that point, Jewher all of sudden wakes up. "Oh, no," she says. "Oh, no."

Sophia was mostly beagle. Not huge. And she just barked when somebody new came in to announce herself.

I said, "That bark is the only word she has in her entire vocabulary; so when she's happy to see you, she'll say that."

Jewher was terrified. I didn't know she'd be afraid of dogs.

It took a little time. I showed Jewher that if she waved at her, Sophia would wave back. Within about two weeks, she was fine with Sophia. She could even take Sophia for walks.

But at first, after everything, and after thirty-six hours of no sleep, imagine the scene: Jewher walks into the house and there's a dog. She was pretty scared. After we got her bags upstairs, she came down, had dinner, then she went back up and she went to sleep.

Meanwhile, as far as we knew, Ilham still was being held.

EVEN WHEN I LIVED at my high school in Beijing, it still was only five minutes away from our apartment. Because he was a university professor, and because the high school and his university belonged to each other, my father also was five minutes away. He'd always come back and stand in front of the window to wait for me at the lunch break—*Just where is my daughter?* He always said that as I came through the door. So I'd see him every day. Our school did not allow us to take phones in, so my family couldn't just call me like that. Sometimes after my brother came back from kindergarten with my stepmom they would stay in front of my school's gate, just to wait for me. They'd stand there for up to an hour, until they would see me. I saw them every day. I never left my family very far away. And then suddenly I was across the world. In Bloomington, Indiana.

I'm not belonging here. How can I start my life here?

The first night at Elliot's, I think I fainted the moment I reached the bed. When I woke up, I looked around. It felt funny. For a moment it was as though it was normal. It was the weekend. The bed was soft like in my home. (Not like the bunk beds at school.) But then I noticed the light when I turned the switch. It was a kind of orange. The lights at my home are fluorescent. More white and blue. So when I saw this color, it just felt strange. And for one second, I couldn't remember what had happened. I looked around the room. Oh yeah, I remembered, I'm in America.

And the first thing I wanted to do when I woke up was to try to call my family.

I came slowly down the stairs. I felt dead. I barely knew where I was.

Elliot and I called. My stepmom answered. She told me that my dad hadn't come back yet.

I just sat there with Elliot, thinking: What is the next step?

# PART TWO

In China, specifically Beijing, some people will treat you as a Uyghur nicer than how they treat Han Chinese. Some will people treat you worse. For the people who treat you nicer, there are two reasons. One is because of your minority nationality—they think it's fresh. They've never seen it before. Second is that you look like a foreigner. They think it's prettier, and they think it's new. Between the two of those, they can want to treat you nice.

But there is an opposite side: many won't treat you as good as how they treat Han Chinese. Because you look different. In any environment, people can't accept a different thing very easily, so they consider us as a different thing. Like different group of people. It makes it hard for them to get along with us very easily. Now I know that sometimes a lot of Han Chinese people have bad impressions of Uyghur people. They see a lot Uyghur people in China who are homeless, or uneducated, and maybe with some little, very small business, like selling cheap kebab on the street. If you don't have a home, then you can't take shower. So some of the Uyghur people they see look dirty, and that is the impression they are left with. They think all the Uyghur are like this. If they see one or two or ten, they think all are like this.

There were two thousand people in my grade at my high school. Including me, there only were three Uyghurs. The two others were boys.

When I was in that school in 2009, the July 5th conflict happened in Xinjiang. So at that time, all Urumqi, the main city, was blocked. In our high schools in China you have to apply, just like college here. The teachers might go to every city to offer the exams, and if the students passed, they could get admission for our high school. But because of all the problems in Xinjiang occurred during exam times, when the teacher went there, everybody was at home because they were afraid. The army was on the streets. So that year, only a few Uyghur people from Xinjiang attended the exams. I think just two or three people passed, and only one of them came. But because my identifications belonged to Beijing, not Xinjiang, I could get in easily.

**Editors**: When you're on the street in Beijing, do people know you're Uyghur?

**Jewher**: Some do; some don't. As I said, they think Uyghur people look dirty. But because I grew up in a family who is educated, I look neat. So, they consider me as a foreigner. Or as a Uyghur student who studied in Minzu University.

**Editors**: Do they consider you Chinese?

**Jewher**: Han Chinese? No, no because I don't look Han Chinese. Say I go shopping. There's a mall in China—Wuxi Mall. A lot of foreigners come to buy things there. And because a lot foreigners come there, the Han Chinese will assume I'm a foreigner, too. They won't think that I'm Uyghur. When I'd go there with my dad, they'd speak English to us. And they'd treat us with a lot of attention. *Oh please come buy this! Come buy that!* They think foreigners are rich. But when we spoke Chinese, they recognized that we were Uyghur, and they started to ignore us. *Oh, buy whatever you want, just pay there.* A total change in attitude.

**Editors**: Do you think of yourself as Chinese?

**Jewher**: I'm from China, from Beijing, but I'm not Han Chinese. I am Uyghur, which is a part of China—one of the 56 different kinds of ethnic groups that include Han. When I was in China, a lot of Uyghur people felt like they were a "second-level citizen." It was hard for them to get a job.

Actually, it happens anywhere—even in America, it happens. But, it's different. It's different because the Chinese government says, "oh, we have to be equal but still…" Whereas in America, when the government says everyone is equal, they mean it. They actually do it. In China it's hard. People pretend to be equal; they say it: we are equal. They say it over and over, but they can't do it. It's hard to do.

So this makes it hard for Uyghur people to get jobs, even if they've graduated from University. It happened to my cousin. She went to school in Beijing and after she graduated, she lived in our home for a year. During that time we got very close. I remember when she tried to get a job. Although she passed the writing exam she needed for the position, she was not accepted for the job. They accepted a Han Chinese man instead. But this Han Chinese man—he was much lower than her: she had better grades, better exam results, better experience. She was so angry. She went back to the interviewer and asked why they chose him over her. The person told her, "don't you know? Don't you really know why?" And then she understood. Growing up Uyghur, you learn to understand this type of talk. It meant: *because you're Uyghur.* That was enough to make the man better than her.

And so, no—I am different than just Chinese. Because implying that I am just Chinese would be saying that all Chinese are treated equally in Beijing, and I watched that not be true.

But what I will say is that in America it's different. Not many people here know Uyghur. But they know I look different. My face, it's not totally American. Yet in my experience people in America don't judge you when they talk to you. They won't change their attitude toward you because you look different, because everyone in America looks different. It doesn't make you lesser.

Here, I don't really feel that people treat you as minority. Because there are so many different kinds of people—not only Uyghurs, but there are also Indians, Mexicans, Koreans, Japanese. There are people from everywhere. Even when you're from another country, you can still be an American. Just like that. And I don't feel like I'm anything wrong here. But in China, even though it's my home, and even though it's where I'm from, I feel sometimes—not always—like I don't belong.

ON MY THIRD DAY in America, I got to Skype with my father for the first time. I learned that he had been detained for one day at the airport, and then he was sent home under house arrest. After three days he was able to talk on the computer. When I first saw his face pop up on the screen, I cried. I cried a lot. And I was nervous. I was nervous that we would be separated forever. He had told Elliot that it was better for me to stay here, in America, and that scared me because I didn't know if he would have to stay in China.

We talked on Skype every day for the next few months. He was worried about me being on my own. I was so young, just eighteen. I was still a little girl and my father was very worried that I wouldn't know how to take care of myself well. That's how fathers are though; they worry about their daughters. So we would Skype and I would tell him everything that I was doing.

*Elliot Sperling*

SOMETIMES SHE ACTUALLY GOT to Skype with friends in Beijing. They didn't know anything about what happened; they just thought Jewher had gone to America to study or something. They didn't know. But being able to communicate restored a kind of normality, such as it could.

Two or three days later I heard her singing. It was the first time. And I thought: *Okay, it's going to be okay.*

Within the week, she even got to like the dog.

At that point it seemed kind of normal. Maybe not normal, but at least it seemed kind of manageable.

A MONTH TURNED INTO months. Elliot helped me to arrange an extension for my visa for school. From February to October. Each month we'd go to Indianapolis to renew my visa.

Because one month Elliot had been busy, I'd gone to the immigration office with another Uyghur. They treated me so bad. *Why you are extending your parole?* The workers thought I was an illegal immigrant.

And once Elliot found about it, he was angry! I'm pretty sure if you were talk to Elliot about this, he would mention this to you. So the next time, before he and I went, he called the State Department. And the State Department called the immigration office. When we arrived in Indianapolis, they treated us so nicely.

*Elliot Sperling*

AND SO DURING THE period in which she was paroled, we needed to get the parole extended; and at that point I was at a conference in California. So I couldn't go with her up to Indianapolis. I told her I'd spoken to people in Washington who said she shouldn't wait for me—she should just go take care of it now. So we arranged for someone to take Jewher up to Indianapolis, because she had to do it at the airport, where they have the CBP station. There, they gave her a big lecture and told her, you're going to have to leave the country in two days or we're going to come for you. And so when I found that out—I'm still in California—again I'm calling State, rather vexed about what happened. State then made the necessary calls. When I came home we went to Indianapolis again. Somebody must have said something to someone, because from there on in they were very polite. In fact, one person asked me, *How did you get involved in this?*

This is only maybe a month or two into it. I'm still interpreting and translating for Jewher. So it's very funny, for some of those with whom we dealt it was sort of like she's the young child, and I'm the big person taking care of her. It often happens when somebody is interpreting for someone else, those for whom the translation is being done sometimes tend make judgments—oh this person (the non-English speaker) probably doesn't know that much. So it took a while to overcome that impression.

One evening when I was speaking with Ilham, we began to talk about Jewher's long-term educational plans. At that point, there was no doubt, *no doubt*, that she was not going to go back to China.

I have to add, because after all of this time here, after speaking out for her father, after writing for her father, under present circumstances she can't go back. I mean she could, but the outcome would not be good. It really wouldn't be good. I wouldn't put any faith in official reassurances and I told Jewher as much.

So very, very quickly, we realized that Jewher was here to stay. And so the first thing was to get her into intensive English classes. I discussed with Ilham the fact that to become a regular student at Indiana University in the future there would be a TOEFL language proficiency requirement. So we went through getting her enrolled in the IEP program, which is only for English. But what they suggested, and what I thought was a good idea, is that Jewher should also take classes. So she did both and sat in on classes. A very good transitional program that was preparing her to become a regular IU student.

Everything had been completely upended in her life. It was completely unexpected. It was a situation in which one world disappears and another begins. What was happening was not what she'd signed up for.

IN SEPTEMBER, I HAD to go to Canada to change my status to an F-1 visa—a student visa—from the J-2 I'd had just to accompany my father. To get this document, you first need to have an I-20 in hand, given to you by the school you are attending. Then you have to leave the country with this I-20, and go to your embassy in Canada or Mexico to get a temporary visa. Next you come back in with that document; it has to be stamped in your passport that you entered the country with that F-1 visa.

Meanwhile, I'd still been doing homework for my university in China because I was expecting to go back. I knew that if I didn't return to school after one month, they would delete my documents at the university. So instead I cancelled my enrollment for the semester in China and took a leave of absence. I applied to Indiana University's language program to take some classes. Indiana would be just for studying language. Then I could go back to my university in China once this all ended.

*Elliot Sperling*

THAT SUMMER, IN 2013, when I went to Beijing, I met with Ilham. At that point, things still seemed manageable. For Ilham, there were little things that were happening that were hints of what was in store. Indeed, some months later, as he was driving with the family, State Security officers rammed his car.

It was things like that until January—where we've been ever since.

When I was meeting with Ilham, I was followed. We were both followed. Not twenty-four hours round-the-clock, but certainly when I would meet with Ilham. For instance, the first couple of times he and I met at the West Gate of Minzu University. They were watching. People had told me it was very common and that some of the people I'd see in stores might be being paid to give information to the police about me, if they saw me going around.

People living in that environment sort develop a kind of "Secret Police-*dar*; a sort of radar about surveillance" Although it's not always meant to be so secret. When it's done so obviously, it seems that they want you to know you're being watched. Most dissidents are aware of the fact that you can never be wholly sure about when or whether you're being watched or not.

People used to ask me whether I was afraid of being followed when I was over there. Mind you, I was never involved in anything that could remotely be considered illegal in any democratic society. Generally, I did not think I was being followed. I know a lot of people who are afraid to meet with certain people there. Even over here they're often afraid to speak out because of what it could do to their prospects of going there. Of course, when you're there, you understand that they can't follow everybody, all the time. So the system exerts its pressure because people don't really know if they're being followed or not. It's very much like "The Anaconda in the Chandelier," that may or may not come down, as described in the well-known article by Perry Link. You never really know, and so many think it best to always err on the side of caution. And so many people modify their behavior.

So, too, the ambiguity is useful in sowing discord. This dissident might be arrested while that one isn't, causing people to think that perhaps the one not arrested has to be working for the authorities? Of course it's an idiotic way of thinking. To be blunt, you're not arrested until you are arrested. Ai Weiwei was not detained until he was detained; Ilham Tohti was not arrested and put on trial for serious crimes until he was arrested and put on trial. It serves the purpose of the authorities to have some people asking why so-and-so is not in prison; to have them thinking that such a person must be working for the government or the Party.

Sometimes factors might work in someone's favor: family background, i.e., having a veteran of the Civil War or better a veteran from Yen'an in the family. But that's still hardly a guarantee and with the current purge of certain figures for "corruption" (something of which those carrying out the purge are in many cases no less guilty) there are fewer safe bets.

On the day I arrived in Beijing, I found out that Ilham had been placed under house arrest. While I wasn't expecting that, I can't say I was really surprised. It was not the first time and it was not the worst thing that the authorities had done to him up to that point. But then later, after I got into town, he let me know that he was no longer detained. And that evening we met for dinner.

But despite the fact that State Security had pulled back, outside the main gate of his housing compound there was a big van with officers inside, obviously there to monitor his movements.

Another night we ate in a restaurant, watched by two otherwise ordinary looking men, wearing shorts and t-shirt, just sitting there. Sure enough, when we left, they left. And where we drove they followed us, pulling up alongside to get a look at me.

But then one night, before I left, I went to his house in the compound. Ilham had some gifts that he wanted me to take back to the U.S., including a laptop for his daughter to use and other things for those who had befriended her since she had arrived all alone in the U.S.

I went up to his place to get the things that he wanted me to take back. As I walked with him into the compound someone came after me asking who I was. This was not the campus gate guard but someone from State Security. Claiming that I was his friend, but wanting to know my name (logic is irrelevant here), we were able to leave him after the possibility of an altercation arose. The campus guard refused to interfere, knowing the man hassling me was State Security. And ultimately the State Security officer didn't do anything further; he seemed to have orders not to have anything too untoward take place in front of a "foreign guest."

After getting the gifts we came back out. This time there was another person from State Security. More muscular, and again asking me who I was. Of course this sort of petty harassment is trivial compared to what people like Ilham have had to put up with in the course of daily life.

And it occurred again, after Ilham dropped me off the next evening for my flight out of China. I was tailed by two people in the airport. They were likely waiting for me to arrive (flight manifests are monitored by the authorities). They were watching while I was in line to check in and then, as I walked around the terminal they were never far behind. I walked to one end and they were nearby (averting their gazes from mine) and at the other end they were there too. When I went to the information counter they followed too. Whenever I turn to look, they're looking somewhere else. This goes on for a while. Finally I go to the area restricted to those with boarding passes, where you descend by escalator to take the airport train to the actual departure area. A lot of people are saying goodbye there. I put my boarding pass into the scanner, and it comes out. The gate opens, and I go in.

And I turn around and the guys are there. So I start waving to them and saying goodbye (in Chinese). "*Zaijian!*" I say, along with everyone else taking leave of family and friends.

Sometimes it seems as though there was a certain inevitability in my becoming involved with the situations of Jewher and Ilham. I had certainly not set out to do so. I certainly knew of Ilham and his work, but I had come to China seeking to know him better or to become friends. This was just something that happened quite naturally. But having become friends, and knowing what he was doing and the tremendous repression to which he was being subjected, there was no possibility of not doing what I did, which was simply to speak out. (And even that was quite slight and insignificant in the larger picture.) But the rights and the wrongs of the situation are very clear, so the question of what to do was an easy one. I've said before that I was never going to change my behavior to accord with authoritarian norms, just for the sake of a visa. And this is the way I still feel.

AFTER A YEAR—WELL, ACTUALLY eight months—went by, I felt like I wanted to stay here, apply to school here. I started to enjoy the life that I had in America. I felt that it "fit me"—how do you say—more "properly"? I felt like I belonged in America. People accepted my perspective. So I decided to stay here and study at Indiana University.

My father was happy about my decision. I still talked to him almost every day. Sometimes I'd lose contact with him because they—the police—took his computer or put him under house arrest. I would Skype him after class, and when the computer wouldn't connect or he didn't respond, I became nervous and worried. I was scared something had happened to him. Being so far away was hard. I could never really know what was going on.

We had this joke when we would talk on Skype. *Uncle Police.* Sometimes we would be talking about my day—what I had to eat, or what homework I had—and we would suddenly hear: *Beep.* Just one sound, and my father would say: "Your Uncle Police has come to join us." He is humorous, my father. He always makes jokes to help me know not to be so nervous or worried.

We knew we were being listened to, so we were always careful about what we said. All we talked about was normal family stuff—how is school, did you make any friends, other things like this.

There was only one thing my father was afraid to let them know about. Only one thing he needed to tell me: don't come back. He was afraid to let them know that because they were forcing him to convince me to go back to China. I didn't know how they thought, the Chinese police. Maybe they thought if I was here, my father wouldn't be afraid anymore. I became a way for them to get to him.

My father said, "If you are there, I feel safer, much safer. Your brothers are little—they won't do anything. They are afraid to do anything to your brothers because they are so little. Nobody would accept it." People would look poorly upon the government if they were to treat children badly. But with me, I was old enough for them to use. So my father told me: "I feel more comfortable with you there. Even though I miss you very much. Because you'll be safe, and get a better education there."

Plus, everybody knows here is better.

Since we couldn't talk about his situation with the government during our conversations, he warned me that if he were ever to get detained, I had to check Twitter or Facebook for information. For three or four months before he got detained, I always thought he was overthinking. I thought that he thinks too much. Too much about bad things. And then it really happened. He was detained, and I realized he wasn't thinking too much. He was preparing me.

He always told me, "Please Jewher, be careful. You have to study hard. You have to."

He always emphasizes this.

He said, "Please study hard. For me."

Like that.

MY FIRST AMERICAN FRIEND was Elliot. I was so reliant on him. And even though I didn't know him before I arrived, I treated him as a dad, as a teacher, as a father, and as an everything. And I was grateful when, right away, Elliot helped to get me enrolled in the International English Program at IU.

I was so nervous the first day I went to classes. How am I going to face a lot of international students from so many different countries? How would I communicate with them?

But at the first session of English classes I was very talkative. Many international students are afraid to talk. But I'm not. I just talk, talk, talk, talk. The first level was pretty easy for me. The teachers told me my English was very good, especially for a Chinese student new to America. I jumped to level four, even though I had hoped for level five.

Soon, a lot of students began to ask me for help. And from there I started to become friends with them. Also, because I'm from China, and because I look different, some of my classmates thought I was interesting. Most those people who I met in those first three of four months are still are my best friends now.

It is hard for me to meet American students, mostly because all of my classmates are international students. As I said, my first and best American friend was Elliot. Second came my American roommate—my first roommate. She was pretty nice. And my third American friend—I mean a real, same-age friend—is my language partner who studies Chinese.

But if it were not for my father's case, I wouldn't know a lot of Americans.

It was cold when I arrived in the US. But when the spring came, and the snow was gone, I thought I might like living here after all.

After one month, I moved into a dorm at IU for a semester—until May. And then during the summer, I lived in another place we called Campus Corner. I went there because they only required a three-month contract. Most asked you to sign for a year. But

I wasn't sure how long I was going to stay. I needed something only for a little, short period. At Campus Corner, they chose the roommates. So I had three roommates that I didn't know before.

I lived in that apartment for three months.

In August, after I went to Canada to change my visa, I decided I'm going to live in America. So I signed a one-year contract for my current apartment.

SOMETIMES I FEEL SO anxious. I want to express my anger, but I can't. If I do like that, people will say, "Ah, look at this: Ilham's daughter is uneducated, blah, blah, blah." Whatever what I do people will comment.

So I dance a lot. I've been dancing for fifteen years, fourteen years. I stopped in my second year of high school. But I've started again since I've been here. Otherwise, I have no way to explode.

I spin fast. Very fast. It makes me forget a lot.

Some people drink to forget. I dance to forget.

There's a Central Asian dance. It's called "Why Are the Flowers So Red." It's very slow. Sad music. A lot of spinning. I love that song. Every time when I dance it, especially the beginning, everything feels like a long time ago. Like something has happened way before us.

My father knows that I love dancing, but actually he doesn't know that I am good at it.

He prefers me to focus on my studies.

He doesn't know that when I dance, I feel much better. Even if I'm tired, I feel happier.

I WASN'T ALWAYS VERY religious. My father wants me to be modern, not so extreme. But when I was here in America, and all these bad things were happening to my family, I thought that maybe if I pray, Allah will listen to my hope and they will help my family. Just like when I dance, when I pray I get inner peace. Especially when I pray during Ramadan. I feel that. When I pray, I feel my heart get cleaner. And I feel safer. I feel like my family is being helped.

I am a modern Muslim. That is what my father wants me to be. He believes it is important to have a Muslim foundation, that this should be the way you live your life. But he believes in being moderate. Like following basic rules. In the Koran, this means treating people nice, and donating money for charity. And helping Uyghur people. My father believes these are important to being a good Muslim.

At the end of the praying, we can say one wish to Allah. Every time I say, "Allah, let my father have a longer life."

Then I say it again in my heart.

I FOLLOWED MY FATHER'S website. Mostly though I checked his blog. I started looking at it ever since I first came to America. Sometimes it was too much pressure for me—it made me worried. Every time when I watched the posts people put up, I felt worried. Not so much because of what my father wrote, but because there were some people who wrote extremely insensitive comments under it; they said things like "I'm going to kill you." Things like that.

At the time I was still a teenager. Maybe not mature enough? I had to always be careful about every word I said. Because everybody in China was watching. Especially the government. If I were to say something wrong, they would put it on my father's head.

So I checked on everything first. Ask my stepmom. Ask Elliot. Ask all of the people I trusted to help me make the correct decisions about how to respond. I always had to apologize for replying late to the people who'd been emailing me and texting me. It's not because I didn't want to reply. It was because I had to think about it over again and again, and ask again and again, just to find the best solution.

On Skype my father would ask me: "Did you do your homework? Do you eat? You have to drink this. You have to eat one banana. You have to eat this, and eggs and milk for breakfast. And then you have to eat this for lunch; you have to do eat like that for dinner."

*Okay, okay.* And then I didn't.

But he'd check.

Sometimes he even woke up in the middle of the night just to check if I was home.

He's strict. But it's just because of how much he cares about me.

**Editors**: Were you still expecting that he would come here?

**Jewher**: Until January, I was still expecting. I still thought he might come. Until that January morning. We were always hoping. I even expected that my brothers might get passports. Until January, I still was expecting . . . But.

I WAS SHOCKED THE first time I heard an American say: "How are you doing?" I thought, *Why do you care how I am doing?*

Or: "What's up?" *Why do you want to know what am I going to do?* When I first came here, and after I figured out what that meant, I felt so stupid. I answered it exactly: What am I going to do is go to the school, and then go to the store. And they'd say: "Okay, Okay, bye!"

It's a lot of cultural differences. When I first came, I am pretty sure I looked so dumb. I didn't know to give tips when I went out to eat. Imagine, I went to one restaurant several times, and I never left them tips. I don't think that they liked me.

I remember being shocked at school the first time a girl held the door for me. What is she doing? In China, if it were a man, it might be little normal. But never a girl. And if she did for some reason, you would know there was something she wanted from you. But here it is so, so normal.

People accepted my perspective here more than in China. My personality is very outgoing. Not like the usual Chinese girls. So I preferred that I could be like that here without feeling different. It didn't feel as obvious.

Still, there was so much to learn about being in a new country. How to cook. I didn't know anything about that. Doing laundry. When I lived at my high school, I saved all my clothing, and took it home to wash it. Here, I had to learn to wash them myself. And who wants to wash the clothing, right?

In China, I had my parents to help me with everything. But since I came here, I quickly had to deal with how to manage my money, my living expenses, finding my apartment, paying rent, paying the utilities.

And I barely even spoke English. A couple of times the power company shut the electricity down when my bill was late, and I didn't have electricity for a few days.

I was stupid; I didn't know how to take care of it online. I had to go far away. Take the bus for an hour to pay my bill. But later I figured out I could just do it online, very easily.

I feel more independent than before.
Yeah.

AFTER DECEMBER, BUT UNTIL January 14th, everything seemed like it was going to be okay. My parents were fine. I was fine.

Money was a little harder—because one dollar here equals six yuan in China. That made a little pressure for my parents. They had to spend 6,000 yuan to give me a 1,000 US dollars. And because of my father's case, he wasn't drawing much of a salary.

But except for that part, everything was pretty fine at that time.

Maybe three months after I'd been here, we were Skyping. When my father drank a little beer, he would open up a little differently. It was like the beer made him tell the truth.

It was midnight there. And he'd turned off the light on purpose because he didn't want me to see he was crying.

It had been a long time since I remembered seeing my father cry. A very long time. He missed me so much. I was my father's child. In China we have a saying that is along the lines of "daughters are a little sweeter."

But because of the screen shining . . .

Yes, I saw him cry. Plus, he sounded so different.

December was the first time I knew of them threatening my father's life. In Xinjiang, my grandma had been sick, so she flew to Beijing to be with my family and to get some medical treatment. Along with my stepmom and my brothers, my father picked up my grandma at the airport. While they were driving back, a car started to come at them, and then crashed into them.

My father got out of the car, pointed at the driver, a secret policeman. "There are children inside," my father screamed. "Children."

"That's what I meant to do. To kill the entire family."

Back at home, my father told a reporter about what had just happened. He wanted the story out there as some kind of evidence. It was the only way he knew to fight against the threat.

I always had stayed with my father more than my mom. Now my father just couldn't get used to life without me. Back in China, he used to always complain that I don't cook for him. I didn't know how. But I learned in the U.S. I would send pictures of my meals to him. He'd say, "You are cooking for everyone except me! I am so jealous."

"I will cook everything for you, everything that you want. Please come."

"Just for your food, I will come."

I really want him to try my food. I want to cook for him.

BUT JANUARY 15TH JUST...

I COULDN'T SLEEP THE night of January 14th (January 15th in China, since they are twelve hours ahead). I didn't know what was happening there—or about to happen.

When I first came here, and I would get sick, I'd call my father. He also would be sick. It was always like that with us. If I caught cold, then maybe he'd have a fever. Always sick at the same time. It's weird.

So that night in January, I didn't do anything unusual before I went to bed. I felt okay. There was nothing to be sad about. But for the whole night I couldn't sleep. I didn't know why. I was rolling. Tossing and turning. For no reason, I would open my eyes. I just didn't know what to do.

I got up and texted my stepmom. But she didn't reply. It made no sense. She shouldn't have been asleep. It was noon in China. Why wouldn't she answer? And actually, it turns out something was happening to my family at that time. Of course, I didn't know. But I did know.

I texted. I called my family a hundred times. They didn't pick up. And . . .

That morning I went to school. I was so tired when I came back, and I wanted to take a nap. I turned off my phone.

There was a knock on my door. It was Elliot. He said he'd been trying to call me.

"I'm sorry," I said. "I turned off my phone to take a nap. I am so tired."

"Your father is detained."

"What?" I wasn't sure I heard right at first. Also, he always jokes with me. "Are you kidding with me?"

I could tell the answer in his face. I grabbed my phone, turned it on, and checked the Internet. It really had happened. All over the news. And it was horrible. Like that. And then...

**Elliot**: Well that's a bit embarrassing, I don't know if Jewher—

**Jewher**: Which one? My house?

**Editors**: When you were sleeping on January 15.

**Elliot**: When Ilham was arrested. And you hadn't been online. So, and I couldn't get you on the phone, so I went to your house.

**Jewher**: Oh, oh yeah.

**Elliot**: And then afterwards you came back to my place do you remember? Yeah? I mean that's a very difficult thing to do. You see, with me and Jewher, whenever we talk we're joking around half the time.

**Editors**: She thought you were kidding.

**Elliot**: Yeah. But I would never joke about something like that. Then we checked on the phone, used the Internet, and there it was. She started to cry. And then she began to repeat, very lowly, a prayer. And from there on in, it was a constant struggle to get information. To find out what we could find out. Either through people I knew, or people she knew, or Ilham's wife. Just trying to find out what was happening. It was very, very difficult because right from the start they wouldn't let anybody see Ilham. Even his lawyer wasn't allowed in. And we didn't even know where he was. We didn't know at first if he was in Beijing, or Urumqi. Or where. At the very beginning nobody knew where he was. It was very, very, very nasty.

I WAS WAITING ALL night. Again, I couldn't sleep. I was waiting for it to be daytime in Beijing, so that I could call when they were awake.

A hundred times. I must have called a hundred times. But they still didn't pick up.

Why? Why? Why?

I knew they detained my father, but why couldn't my stepmom pick up the phone?

I was so afraid that they did something to the rest of my family. I was especially worried about my brothers. Because I'd read in the news that they were together when the police arrested my father at our apartment. I was so worried.

I heard nothing for almost a week. But then my stepmother found a way to contact me. It was because my brother's iPad was under his pillow. That was where he'd hid it, under his pillow on the top level of the bunk bed. He didn't want my father to see he was playing games.

The police didn't see that one. They got everything else. All the phones. The computer. Everything except that iPad. And that's how my stepmom finally reached me to tell me that she and my brothers were safe. By that iPad. Otherwise, they wouldn't have been . . .

I don't know what I would have done.

# PART THREE

SOMETIMES I WONDER HOW people could go in and do that to a family. Those policemen were acting under orders. Communism. They were told to go in and detain my father. But I'm pretty sure they weren't ordered to push him into the couch or anything like that. And I'm pretty sure my father didn't fight back so they didn't need to do that. My father isn't that type of person.

The government says my father is a terrorist. But my father did not hurt anybody. He was just trying to help. Trying to be a moderate voice toward finding a peaceful solution to this longstanding issue between the Han and the Uyghur people.

Do the people in charge really have a sense for what is . . . *who* is . . . terrorizing who?

My STEPMOTHER WAS AT work. My father was at home
with my brothers. I only know this next part from what I read in
an article, but apparently my grandma had decided to go out for
a walk. While she was out, two Uyghurs probably working for the
police approached her, and started talking with her in Uyghur.
Somehow they led her away somewhere. She always has been
very trusting. When I heard this I was so angry. What were they
going to do with an old woman—especially one who didn't even
speak Chinese? I've never asked her the details. Everything about
this time upsets her too much.

My father was taking a nap when they burst into the house,
breaking down the door. According to my brother, there were
more than twenty police. Twenty to forty.

The family apartment in Beijing was small, almost the same
size as my apartment in America; the one I share with just a
single roommate. And all those men came in and filled the
whole space.

"What is going on?" my brother began screaming and crying.
"What is going on?"

When my father stood up, the police pushed him down onto
the sofa.

My brother had never seen my father so scared. My father is
more strict with him; it is rare for my father to seem weak. So this
moment really shocked my brother.

Meanwhile the neighbors, hearing all the noise, called my
stepmom and told her to come home.

Grandma had come to Beijing from Xinjiang to go to the
hospital because she hadn't been feeling well. So the whole time,
as my stepmom rushed home from her work at the library at
Minzu University, she was thinking it was my grandma that was
in trouble.

When she came into the apartment my brothers were
alone.

"Where is your grandma? Your father?"

To the first question, they shrugged; they figured she was out for a walk. To the second, they told her the police had taken him away.

They came back again, the police. The first time, they'd grabbed my father and took all the documents they could find. The second time they came at night and took every electronic device they could find.

Two times they scared my brothers.

Two times they were traumatized.

AFTER MY FATHER WAS detained in January, I worried about some of the Han Chinese friends I had in Bloomington. I didn't want them or their families to get into trouble for knowing me—especially because the news in China was so one-sided about my father. I'm pretty sure some of my friends talked to their families back home about what they should do. If I were them, I would have done the same thing: "Oh, it turns out my friend is involved in something very political. Parents, should I keep talking with Jewher?" I think it was responsible. You know, just as I was, they were responsible for their family, too. They had to be worried that it could influence what happened to them in China.

I understood. But at the time some of these people were my best friends. I was a little sad.

There were four months when I didn't have a roommate. When my current roommate, who is Han Chinese, inquired about the room in my apartment, I told her, "I'll give you a month to think about it. Then re-think it. And then talk to your family. If you decide, you'd like it, then feel free to come. I'd be so happy to have you as my roommate. Because we'd be partners."

Exactly one month later she texted me: "Is your room still available?"

I said, "So you don't care?"

"I don't think you are doing something wrong."

That's what friends are like, I think. Later when my father was sentenced, and my roommate's parents saw the news on TV in China, they told my roommate she should stay with me and comfort me. I was so sad at the time, but this gesture was so moving.

WHEN THEY TOOK MY father away, that was when things began to change for me. I'd just been starting to make a life for myself here in America, and then that happened. My life changed all over again.

In China, things were even more difficult for my family. Our neighbors stopped talking to my stepmom. My brothers' friends didn't want to play with them anymore. They were just kids. They didn't do anything.

For a while my whole family was under house arrest. They weren't allowed to leave the apartment. And even after the government took them off house arrest, my family had between four and eight guards with them at all times.

They would sleep outside our house during the nighttime.

The guards went with my brothers to school. What were two little boys going to do? I don't understand why the guards needed to do this to them. They were so small!

The guards went with my stepmother to work and stayed outside her building all day. She doesn't even speak Chinese. Just Uyghur. So she could also do no harm. But they made sure she didn't leave. Then when she was done working, they would follow her home. It was like this. All the time.

One time people came from the American embassy department to bring food, but the guards wouldn't let them in. It was so hard for anyone to help.

At the local park, the guards ran all around, right behind my brothers. And so my brother says, "Ahh, don't they feel tired?"

But they don't ever seem to get tired.

For the first month, I thought the government was just threatening my father. I thought they'd detained him just to scare him, to get him to shut up. But then we didn't hear for him for another month.

And then another.

For six months he couldn't contact anybody. That was totally illegal.

Legally speaking, if you are a political prisoner, they can detain you at most for three months before they have to let you speak to your family or your lawyer. That is why I waited until March to act. I waited to give the government a chance, and also a chance for myself—to hold on to hope that things will be all right.

But then March came and still no one had heard from my father.

That's when I knew it was for real. They didn't care about giving my father his rights.

I decided to get involved in his case from America. Somehow.

**Jewher**: In the United States I don't feel watched. I don't feel like the Chinese government can get to me here. But when I go to New York, and I pass by the Chinese embassy, and I think of how my father was treated, I feel cold. On my skin.

**Editors**: Goosebumps?

**Jewher**: Goosebumps? No, I feel on my skin… (*rubs her hand against her forearm*)

**Editors**: Chills?

**Jewher**: Yeah, I feel like that. And all down my back. Here, I feel cold. Chills.

WE WERE ALL WAITING and trying to get information from my father's lawyer. Nobody could speak with him. We didn't even know where he was.

We were constantly refreshing the websites to find new information. But everyday it was the same news. The same until then we found out that my father's students were also detained. Ridiculous.

My uncle—my father's brother—is a police-man. He was trying to find out for us. Every way he asked. *Where is my brother? Where is my brother?* Everybody said don't get involved. Please, don't get involved.

That was the only thing that we knew.

And then finally my uncle learned where my father was being held. At least we knew he was alive; that was the best news to find out.

I had been so worried that they would hurt him. You see, my father is not sick but he has a very weak body. He's been so tired for so long. It had been a long time for him to be so stressed.

PEOPLE HAD BEEN CALLING and calling. Reporters. Lawyers. Private organizations. They all wanted to talk to me. But I was careful to remain quiet.

Then in March, I accepted my first interview. It was with Voice of America, VOA. It was important to me to keep my interviews personal, not political. I just wanted to talk about my father's detainment and how wrong it was. That is why I started accepting interviews: for my father. The political side of things— talking about those issues—I thought would hurt my father more than it would help him. And I was just a teenager—I didn't know anything about Xinjiang. I didn't know what was going on. I only knew what had happened to my father. This first interview though, with VOA, was all political. They kept asking me: "How do you feel about Xinjiang, blah, blah, blah?" I told them I couldn't give them an answer.

It's not that I didn't care about the other people were affected by the conflict in Xinjiang. I did care about how other people were doing, but not at that moment. In that moment, I was most scared for my father, and I wanted to act in ways that I thought could help him.

MY FATHER HAD TOLD me not to get involved in politics. The reason my father is in trouble with the government is because of his involvement with politics. I had to always be careful about what I was saying because everybody in China was watching. Especially the government. If I were to say something wrong, they would put that on my father's head. If I spoke about those things—about the Uyghur people and things like that—then the Chinese government was going to say to my father, "Ah, your daughter is also political, so you must have had something to do with this." So I was careful in my interviews. I didn't want my words to get twisted.

It is scary because the government can make anything fit what they want it to. So if I didn't answer anything political, then they couldn't change my words.

I get a lot of bad feedback from the Uyghur community for not using my position as Ilham Tohti's daughter to pick up in politics where he left off. One woman called and left a message on my answering machine and said, "Your father is doing all these things to help the Uyghur people, why are you not?"

I ignored her message. She didn't understand. I was trying to help my father. What she was doing—what people like her were doing—was making his situation worse. They thought they were doing the right thing. I know in their hearts they thought they were helping my father, but some of the things they did had bad effects on him.

I didn't know these Uyghurs who were calling. I don't know who they worked for, why they were here, or what their political reasons were for staying here. I didn't know anything about them. So I was afraid. Talking to them could be seen as evidence against my father.

Think about it: my father is trying to say that he worked independently, that he wasn't a "leader"—because being a "leader" means that he could be involved with separatism. He is trying to tell the government that he doesn't have any overseas relationships with Uyghur world organizations. And then, all of the sudden, if I am involved with these organizations, the government won't believe my father. *If Jewher is working with Uyghur world organizations, then so are you.*

This is a risk I don't want to take. So I don't care about the negativity I receive from Uyghurs here. I just care about my father.

I hope they can understand that.

With father and brother (2012)

ALL TOLD IT MIGHT *have been only a half-hour. But the ride seemed longer than it was. Perhaps because we all were a little tired. And perhaps some of it had to do with the intensity of the morning's interviews, particularly for Jewher.*

*We'd eaten lunch earlier at Mei Wei on S. Grant Street. There, Jewher had ordered for us off the Chinese menu (as opposed to the menu reserved for American diners, which had the more familiar Chinese-American dishes). Afterward, we strolled downtown, walking off some of the lunch. And then we made our way on to the campus touring among the recently arrived freshman, and then, finally, back to the car. It was Jewher who suggested the drive.*

*Lake Monroe, actually a reservoir within the Hoosier National Forest, is reputed to be largest lake in Indiana. Once land belonging to the Miami Indians, in 1960, the Army Corps of Engineers flooded the basins of Monroe, Jackson, and Brown counties, and dammed Salt Creek south of the area to create it as the main water supply for Bloomington. But additionally, Lake Monroe became a major recreational area, and also among other things, included the state's only federally protected wilderness area. It was this destination we were heading, as we drove south on 37 out of town. Nearing the lake area, Jewher said to slow down. She thought the left turn was close. Then she said never mind. It was further ahead. Despite many possible paths down to the lake, she was looking for a specific one.*

*When we turned onto the long drive toward the area's parking lot, the road narrowed. Poplar and ash trees (just to name a few of the identifiable ones) stretched out of a covering of low bushes that climbed moderately inclined hills. They surrounded us. Getting out of the car, in front of us we saw a lake as grand as any infinite seeming body of water, and a blue so perfect you would think you were making it up. Behind us was the forest. The area felt less like a place one escapes to, and more like a place in which one retreats from.*

*We walked to a dock empty of people and boats. It was slatted, and even though the dock was pillared into the lake's bottom, the movement of the water's surface suggested the pier was swaying* with the ripples. The weather had been brisk in Bloomington that day, but here, at Lake Monroe, the sun was shining, and when we sat on the dock, we all laid back, getting beneath the breeze until it was just sunlight warming us.

"I came out here after I heard about my father's arrest," Jewher told us. "I just came out here to be quiet." She said that since then it has become her spot to disappear from all the noise of her world. "It makes me feel peaceful."

For the next hour or so, we all lay on the dock. It was one of the few times of the weekend when any one of us in some combination wasn't talking. And, almost at lake level, beneath the wind but blanketed by the sun, surrounded by hills of trees, it was one of the few moments when we could remember that we don't always have to be subjects to the world, but that we can be part of it.

# PART FOUR

I DIDN'T KNOW HOW to start helping my father. I didn't know anyone here in America, other than Elliot. I wasn't sure yet who I could trust.

I could take interviews, but I didn't feel that this was enough. They wouldn't reach anyone in China because the government blocks that kind of news.

So many people online were trying to convince the Chinese government to release my father. But they didn't even care. They even ignored a letter the State Department sent to the Xi Jinping. The government just returned it. They didn't open the letter.

So I kept thinking of new ways to get involved. I knew I felt more comfortable talking about my father's case with Americans. Not because I don't like Uyghurs—of course I do, I am Uyghur—but because I was really worried about how the Chinese government would take my involvement with foreign Uyghurs.

Then I thought about Washington. I knew this was the central location for government in America. I knew that important people were there, important people that could help my father.

And then you got in touch with me in February or March, based off of your working with Scholars at Risk, offering to help with the trip—setting up meetings, going with me, and so on. Elliot knew of the good work of Scholars at Risk, so he told me it was a good organization. And when we first spoke with all of you by phone, and I learned that most were undergraduates; I felt like I could trust you. I believed you only wanted to help.

In Washington, D.C.

WHEN WE ARRIVED IN Washington, our planes came at the same time—but to different terminals! I remember talking to Adam on the phone saying, "I'm here," but I wasn't sure where *here* was. There weren't many people around, and it all looked kind of the same. I didn't know how to say where I was. It was my first time in Washington. I said to Adam that I was wearing black. But I had no idea what any of you looked like.

On the cab ride to the hotel, everything outside was so beautiful. The buildings and monuments lit up in the sky.

IN THE MORNING, WHEN we met in the hotel lobby, I was so nervous and confused. Even though we'd gone over everything about the upcoming meetings the night before, and it all made sense, once it was time to go do it, I didn't know what to say!

I had never talked to government before. The entire concept—of being able to speak to important government people—really confused me.

I didn't know how to talk about my father. I think this was the hardest part. Before I hadn't been very vocal about my father's politics. Now I was going to go speak to the American government about my father's situation in China and about his politics.

What kind of questions were they going to ask? They are U.S. representatives. I can't refuse to answer the question if they ask something in which I'm not comfortable.

What should I do?

I knew I would just have to say it and say it and say it. And then maybe, because America is one of the strongest countries in the world, they would give some pressure to China.

Oh please work, I thought.

But I didn't know what to say, or really how to trust. Government had never wanted to help my family before.

THERE ARE TWO MEMORIES I have of the first meetings:

First was at U.S. Senator Donnely's office, from Indiana. We met with one of his staff people. As walked up the hill to his building, everybody kept saying it would be pretty simple. They will ask you some questions, then you can tell them. But when we got in there, everybody was silent. Nobody asked me questions.

How should I start? I didn't know what to say. Adam was looking at me. I remember exactly how he was looking at me. And then he nodded for me to start.

I felt so weird. I didn't know how to organize my language. It's very hard for international students to just talk like that. I felt like I forgot all my English. How should I start with it? How should I explain? How should I finish? How should I have a conclusion?

My heart was jumping actually like *pft pft pft*. It was really, really beating.

"Well, my name is Jewher." That's how I started.

But it was when we went to Congressman Young's office on the other end of the Capitol that I most remember. It was in the Longworth Building, a grand interior with beautiful white marble. Very official. And very fancy. And there I was. I just walked in through the security checkpoint, and I was going up to the office of a U.S. Congressman. I was so surprised. In China they won't let you in. It's hard, anyway. In a similar situation in Shanghai there are 300 cars. 300 soldiers. They door is guarded by men with the guns, and only high-level people can reach the government. But in the Longworth Building, here we were—ordinary, normal people, and we could just get in.

At that moment, I felt like these people are going to help us, because this is the kind of government who you can get contact, who can listen to people—really listen to people—and who can really help people.

AT THE CECC (THE Congressional-Executive Commission on China) meeting I started to see how people here knew about my father and about the Uyghur situation in China. Lawrence Liu and Amy Reger were a big part of this. Amy spoke Uyghur and that gave me some comfort; plus, she was so kind. And Lawrence, he was really nice. He was so helpful in getting us the meeting. Plus he was Chinese. I liked that. We were there to talk about the possibility of my testifying before the CECC. It was something I wanted to do, in order to help my father. There had been some talk about it earlier. Elliot and the State Department had thought it would be the best way for me to tell the story of what had happened.

At the meeting, people told me about what would happen at the testimony. I would have a set amount of time to read a statement. There would be some questions. Senator Sherrod Brown would chair it. They told me about other daughters who had testified. They explained me there would be other people testifying too. And they also told me that everything I would say would be in the public record. I mostly was worried about my father, about what testifying would do to him. I asked Amy if there would be reporters from China there. There would be. Lawrence added that because it was a public hearing, they couldn't control who came. But they could keep me away from people I didn't want to speak with. I could have your students with me. Still, I was nervous that this would hurt my father. The reporters could fix up my words and make it seem like I was talking politics and blame what I was doing in America on my father, even though he had no part in it. This worried me the most.

We talked about it for almost an hour. And then I decided I would do it. Why? I think because Elliot told me it was okay, and everyone at the CECC told me it was okay. I started to believe that they were right. It was the best way I had to help my father.

At the CECC meeting with Ashley and Alexi

I BEGAN TO TRUST the people who told me that what I was doing would only help my father. Sophie Richardson at Human Rights Watch was a big part of this. We met with her right after the CECC. (And I also learned that she would be testifying with me, as well.) Sophie told me that the more we talked about these things, the closer the world would be watching China's actions, and then the less likely they would be to harm my father. I hoped this was true.

She also told me to be confident, and to keep asking for what I want to help my father. Our next stop would be the State Department. I thought that would be a good place to start.

When I saw Sophie, I thought: In the future, I want be like her. She said she'd been to China. She knew about China. And her personality was really like my father's. I liked her a lot. I liked how she talked so much like my father. And I really understood that speaking at the hearing could only help him.

I was feeling more and more confident.

Meeting with Sophie Richardson at Human Rights Watch

AT THE STATE DEPARTMENT, I was so surprised. How could these people from another country know about my father? How do they know? I didn't know my father was so famous.

The entire room was filled. At a long table, we were meeting with people from Democracy, Rights, and Labor, and some people from the China desk. Later, the Assistant Director of the China desk would be coming in also.

There were so many important people there. I remember Scott Busby telling me that this was an important case, especially because my father was a moderate voice, something that was needed at this time to make peace between the Han Chinese and the Uyghur people. And then the director told me that Secretary John Kerry was very concerned about the case. She wanted me to know that it was being taken very seriously at the State Department.

Another woman, Susan O'Sullivan, said, "I just met your stepmother in China."

My first feeling was, *I'm so jealous; I wish I could meet with her too.* But I just answered, "Oh, really."

She said, "Your stepmom is very brave." And she is. I'm very proud of her. She doesn't really know to speak Chinese. She's a very traditional, religious Uyghur woman. And she's really young. Yet she keeps standing for my father. I know it's really hard for her to do that—to be so public. For traditional woman in our culture, you have to keep quiet. Many other women would maybe just sit there and cry all day and say, *oh what am I gonna do.* When she and I had first started chatting on Skype, I'd said, "I'm so proud of you. Thank you." But she got angry. She'd replied, "Why do you say thank you? I'm not someone out of this family. Why do you say thank you? We are family."

At the State Department, I was scared at first, but not like I had been in the beginning of the day. I knew what to say, and I felt good about saying it. Adam didn't have to look at me this time. But I kept thinking about what Sophie had said—to ask for help for my father. At the Human Rights Watch office, I had told

Sophie about how the police were following my little brothers everywhere. To school. To play. Everywhere. They are just little children. They have done nothing. And then I thought that maybe that is what I could ask for. To ask someone to ask the Chinese police to let my brothers be. But then the meeting broke up. However, we still agreed to wait a little bit longer. To meet with the Assistant Director from the China desk.

He came in about ten minutes later. With him were two men, one who had met my father. The Assistant Director expressed concern, and wanted to assure me that this was something he was very involved in.

Time was going away. I needed to ask.

When the meeting ended, and I was shaking everyone's hands, I knew this was my moment. When the Assistant Director approached me, I looked him in the eye. I made sure to. He smiled. I thought, here it is. The moment when I really can help my family. I asked, "Can you do me a favor?"

"Anything."

I told him about the guards following my brother and how wrong it is. I told him they are just little boys and they do no harm. "If you have a way, could you ask about getting the guards removed?"

He nodded. He was thinking. "Yes," he finally said. "I can do that. You have my word."

We ended the day meeting at the office of Senators Whitehouse and Reed from Rhode Island. This is important because eventually they would co-write a letter to the Chinese Ambassador, calling on China to release my father.

# United States Senate
WASHINGTON, DC 20510

April 9, 2014

His Excellency Cui Tiankai,
Ambassador of the People's Republic of China
Embassy of the People's Republic of China
3505 International Place, N.W.
Washington D.C. 20008

Dear Mr. Ambassador:

We write to express our concerns about the detention of Ilham Tohti, a prominent professor of economics at the Central Minorities University in Beijing. This case was brought to our attention by students from Roger Williams University through their association with Scholars at Risk.

On January 15, 2014, Professor Tohti, who has advocated human rights for China's ethnic Uighur citizens, was detained on alleged charges of separatism. Additionally, police reportedly raided his family home, and seized computers, cell phones, passports, and other documents – including his teaching materials and student essays. It is also reported that Professor Tohti has not been permitted consultation with his lawyer, that his family's safety continues to be threatened, and that his bank accounts have been frozen. Additionally, Professor Tohti has a history of health problems and his present health condition is unknown.

We share the concerns raised by the U.S. State Department about Professor Tohti's case, including that his detention "appears to be part of a disturbing pattern of arrests and detentions of public interest lawyers, Internet activists, journalists, religious leaders, and others who peacefully challenge official Chinese policies and actions." Human Rights Watch has stated that there is no publicly-available evidence of Professor Tohti engaging in any form of speech or behavior that could be objectively considered as inciting violence or unlawful action.

As we continue to strengthen the bilateral relationship between our two countries, we urge you to promote internationally-accepted standards of due process, free expression, and freedom of association, which are consistent with China's international human rights commitments. In this vein, we ask you to release Professor Tohti from detainment, and to ensure that Professor Tohti and others like him receive the protections and freedoms that they deserve.

Thank you for your attention to this important matter.

Sheldon Whitehouse
United States Senator

Jack Reed
United States Senator

Cc: The Honorable Max Baucus, United States Ambassador to the People's Republic of China

IT IS A RULE in our family to always greet each other and say goodbye together at the door. If any family member is going out, to school, the store, whatever, every other family member stands in front of the door to say "goodbye." My father says this is how you keep the family connection together, how you keep the family strong.

My youngest brother, he got used to this. Especially, he got used to waiting for me on Fridays, when I would come home from school for the weekend. Every Friday for a month after I went to America, he would sit at the door and wait for me to get home from school. He didn't understand America. He thought the whole world was China. "Where is my sister?" he would say. "Where is Jewher?"

It is a sad feeling to know I can't talk to my father any more. Before, he was always there. Even with me in America, I could Skype him and he would help me through things. And I would help him through things. And now he isn't there. It's a very sad feeling.

When I first got to the U.S., I thought of myself as a regular international student. I'll study, and then maybe I can go back in the summer break or the winter break. I always had hope. But now I am here, and I am forced to stay, because going back to China isn't an option. You have no choice then; everything is different.

With my father's suitcase, I have a pair of my little brother's underwear. I stole them when he was two years old. I know it sounds so silly. But they smell like him.

I wonder if he still sits there and waits.

# PART FIVE

ON APRIL 8TH, I was scheduled to travel to Washington, D.C. to testify on behalf of my father in front of the Congressional-Executive Commission on China (CECC). I would be telling my personal history with my father and all that I had witnessed. I would plead for his release, which I wanted more than anything. I knew there would be Chinese reporters sitting there and staring at me, trying to make me uncomfortable. But I told myself I wouldn't be afraid. Maybe nervous, but not afraid. Because I wouldn't be doing anything illegal or wrong. I remembered that:

- I am here with a legal status.
- I am here to study.
- I only speak about my father.
- I don't talk political.
- I am only a teenager.
- I am not an expert in Xinjiang—I live in Beijing. I grew up there.
- I won't say anything wrong.
- I only will tell what I see.
- Because I only will be telling the truth, they can't do anything to me. They can't have any reason to.

As long as it was the truth, I would not be afraid.

I flipped through the testimonies and articles over and over again. I was so afraid I would say something wrong. This was the biggest step I had made so far. I was going to speak live, broadcasted, for China to see.

I only had two weeks to write and practice my testimony speech. Plus it was right during midterms.

*Great.* The most important thing I am doing for my father is falling during all my exams!

So busy. So busy. My father would be mad that I was putting him above schoolwork.

I did my exams, of course. And I did well. I had to do well, because if I failed my exams, then it would affect my visa status; I could be kicked out of the U.S. and be forced to go back to China. I couldn't let that happen. I had to keep good attendance and good grades. Between it all—I was so nervous.

But thank goodness for Elliot. He helped me with the testimony. We made an outline, and I started to write a statement. But I couldn't finish it. Elliot helped me gather my thoughts and say everything I wanted to say.

The statement had to be five minutes, which may seem like not a lot of time, but to me, it was a long time to speak in English. I was so worried I would mess it up.

But I just thought about the truth; everything I'd write and testify to would be the truth. Remembering that made it much easier for me to write the statement.

I wrote about what had happened to my family since the Urumqi riots in 2009.

I wrote about what kind of person my father is, how kind he is.

Only on the night before the testimony did I finish writing. We printed it out in the morning of the testimony before I left to board the plane in Indianapolis.

Can you imagine that? It was such a busy, short time.

I WANTED TO DANCE or cook to relieve some of the stress. But I was too busy; I didn't have time. It was like all of the sudden I was on the plane. All alone. Preparing to testify in front of the world.

*Elliot Sperling*

JEWHER WAS VERY NERVOUS about speaking in public in English. *Very* nervous. This was a huge thing for her. Having had the experience of speaking in public in languages other than English, I understood how she felt. Every little mistake seems magnified a thousand times. However, she would really need to do this and she understood that. I said to her, although this is not something you've chosen, you have become a spokesperson. And people are looking to you.

Before she was due to testify we had, at IU, the premiere showing of the documentary film, *The Dialogue*—about Wang Lixiong's efforts to create dialogue over Tibet between the Dalai Lama and Chinese intellectuals, as well as through inter-ethnic dialogue. The last fifteen or twenty minutes of the film involves Ilham. He is shown at the athletic field at Minzu University. Earlier in the film we see Wang Lixiong explaining his means of promoting dialogue to Ilham Tohti, which, of course fits the context of Ilham's website which was specifically aimed at getting a dialogue started between Uyghur and Chinese.

Although I would introduce the film, I told Jewher she'd need to say something afterward.

So we worked on what she could say. When she got a bit worried, I just kept reminding her, "Consider this preparation for public speaking."

And she did a good job. She really did a *very* good job.

So next we worked on her statement for the CECC testimony.

I FLEW INTO WASHINGTON early on April 8th. I was alone on the plane for one hour.

Amy Reger from the CECC picked me up at the airport. Once in the city, we still had one hour before I need to be at the hearing at the Russell Senate Office Building. It was hard to stay still. So we walked around the White House and other government buildings. She showed me a little bit. Anything not to think about what I was about to do. And I told that to Amy. I said please don't talk about the hearing. "I'm so nervous about it; please don't tell me anything about how terrible it's going to be."

Amy said, "Don't be nervous. You'll be great."

Next, we went down to Union Station—the train station, where we met Alexi and Jennifer, my two students friends who just had flown down from Rhode Island. I'd wanted them there. I even wanted to them to sit next to me at the table when I testified. Of course they couldn't, but Amy and Lawrence arranged for them to be behind me. Just seeing them at the train station, as we ate Indian food, and knowing they would be sitting so close me feel more comfortable. Like I had more support. Especially because Elliot was not able to come.

We walked up to the Senate building, the four of us. All girls. I carried an H&M bag that held my charger, and other things I'd traveled with for the day. I walked in, trying to feel very normal. But I was afraid someone might recognize me; someone who wanted to make something more political out of my testimony. But I was just there for my dad. Ahead was a Uyghur man that Amy pointed out. She said if I didn't want to talk, I should keep my head down, be quiet and walk past him while she spoke with him. It was like a movie, the remaining three of us walking past, pretending that I am not Jewher Ilham; instead just a girl with an H&M bag going into the senate building. As I walked by him, he and Amy were talking a little. The Uyghur guy said, "Oh, I am going to watch Ilham's daughter talk."

Ack!

I moved even faster, just to make sure that he didn't recognize me. It was just easier. Like I said, for me this testimony was about my father, not Uyghur groups and my representing them. I didn't want to be rude. It's just what it was for me.

Once inside the building, Amy asked if I wanted to go into the hearing room early, just to see how it looked.

"Are there are other people there?" I asked.

"Yes, the audience already is there."

"No, no, no. I'm not going in then."

"It's okay. And we will walk you in later. That way nobody will come up to disturb you."

"Thank you," I said. "Thank you."

We went into a back room. Alexi and Jennifer went out to find their seats. It seemed like time was going both slowly and quickly. I met with a couple of reporters. So many people wanted to talk with me, and I wanted to be helpful, but I also wanted to have some quiet. And then as it was getting closer to the time, the chairman of the committee, Senator Sherrod Brown, came back to meet me. When we shook hands, I thought, *Wow, I am shaking hands with a senator in America.*

Five minutes before the hearing was set to start, I was led to the hearing room. I didn't look at anyone. I was afraid to have any eye contact. Just walk straight, I said to myself.

I was sat at the table. All of the audience was in back of me. I couldn't see anybody except the senators. At the table with me were the other witnesses—Sophie Richardson from Human Right Watch, and Donald Clarke, a professor who spoke Chinese very well. Also testifying on Skype was Teng Biao, a human rights lawyer. Directly behind me was a translator for me to ask whenever I didn't understand anything. And though I couldn't see them, I knew that Alexi and Jennifer were just over my shoulder.

My hands were shaking.

*Oh my god,* I said to myself. I'm sitting here with the people from government. That's so strange for me. It's certainly not the life that I'd wanted before, or at least that I'd meant to have before. But now I'm here, and I have to do it. I have to confront.

I had my prepared statement in front of me. Senator Brown was in charge of the committee. Along with him were Representatives Robert Pittenger and Tim Walz. And at 3:38, Senator Brown began the hearing. As he made his introduction, followed by Representative Pittenger, I got more and more nervous. I knew that once they were finished, I would be the first person to testify. At least I had my statement prepared. But it was the idea of follow-up questions that worried me. I was nervous about saying something wrong. Some of that was being concerned about my English, but also, because I knew the Chinese government would be watching (in fact, I was told they probably had representatives in the hearing room), and I knew they would catch anything I said referring to Uyghurs, and try to do to me what they did to my father. I was afraid they'd say, *she is just like her father. Her dad would say that.* That would not be good for my family.

Senator Brown had just finished welcoming the other witnesses, ending with Sophie Richardson, when I heard him say my name. "Ms. Ilham, welcome. If you would begin your testimony. Thank you."

With the page in front of me, I began to read:

*Hello. My name is Jewher Ilham and I am a student at Indiana University. I'm grateful for this opportunity to appear here and speak about the suppression of dissent in the People's Republic of China as I have personally experienced it.*

In that moment, I might was as well have been reading Spanish or French. *Just don't make a mistake. Just don't make a mistake.*

*Over a year ago, I set out to accompany my father, Ilham Tohti, to the United States, where he was to be a visiting scholar at Indiana University. I was to stay for a month. On February 2, 2013, preparing to depart China, my father and*

*I were detained. Due to a police error, I was allowed to leave.
My father was held, beaten, and forbidden from leaving
China, all for writing about abuses of civil and religious
rights. My father, Ilham Tohti, is a well-known economist
and writer based at Central Minzu University in Beijing and
an advocate for the human rights of the Uyghur people.*

I was thinking, "I can't read." It was like I was trying to remember
how. And then I remember thinking, "Oh, come on. I can read."

*I'm not an academic expert on Xinjiang nor on China's
politics, but I have observed the impact of repressive
Chinese policies on my own family. 2013 was not the first
time my father had been detained and his family harassed.
After serious clashes in Xinjiang in 2009 left many people
dead and a significant number "disappeared," my father
worked to get their names and cast a spotlight on China's
repression of Uyghur grievances.*

*As a result, my family was removed from their
residence and moved around for one month. Our phones
and computers were confiscated. In April 2011, my father
and grandmother were forcibly sent to Guangzhou for a
week.*

*In December 2011, I returned home from school one
day to find an empty home. My stepmother, my father, and
my brothers had been sent to Hainan for two weeks. In
2012, the authorities blocked my brother from registering
for school or having a passport. The university also
canceled my father's class for one semester. His website was
sometimes shut down.*

I'd made it through the first step; the most important step for me.
I knew I could keep going.

*In the fall of 2013, state security personnel rammed my
father's car and told him they would kill everyone in our*

family. But the worst happened after January 15 of this year. A large group of police took my father away without any due process. We had no information about him. His lawyer was denied contact with him. On January 25, the government announced accusations against him, including inciting separatism and hatred of the country, and praising terrorists.

Anyone who knows my father realizes how false these charges are. My father never speaks about separatism. By arresting my father, China has driven Uyghurs to understand that their justified grievances cannot get any sort of hearing. Today, my father is in the Urumqi Municipal Prison, but no one can visit him.

The Chinese state often metes out collective punishment to a prisoner's family. My stepmother has no access to family funds in my father's bank account. She and my young brothers are monitored 24 hours a day. Police sleep outside their door at night and keep watch there during the day.

Phone calls to my stepmother are monitored, making it difficult for her to communicate with me. She may lose her employment due to my father's political imprisonment. My oldest brother has become withdrawn and introverted. Having witnessed our father being taken away, he now has nightmares.

Finally, there are some students of my father who have been arrested and imprisoned too, with very little known as to their whereabouts. China has imprisoned a dissident intellectual whose sole crime was advocating human rights and equitable treatment for the Uyghur people.

I am heartened that the Congressional-Executive Commission on China has taken an interest in my father's case and is seeking to learn more about the facts of his imprisonment.

Thank you.

Phew. Finished.

Next the lawyer Teng Biao testified via Skype. Then Professor Clarke. Then Sophie Richardson. For the whole time, I didn't know where should I put my eyes. Where should I look? I glanced at the TV screen in the right side of the room that was showing the hearing, and I noticed I could see the backs of the audience. That made me too nervous. So I turned to the other side, but there was another screen. With the same view.

I just looked down at my sheet of notes. I didn't know what I should do.

I listened. Tried to take notes. And tried to figure out what I still didn't understand very well.

After Sophie Richardson delivered her prepared statement, Senator Brown, the chairman, looked over to me.

**Chairman Brown**: *Ms. Ilham, thank you again for your testimony. You had said that no one can visit your father. Do you know how he's doing, and do you have thoughts on what we can do to help him?*

**Jewher**: *Until now I didn't get any news about how he is doing because nobody can visit him. And I'm really grateful for what you have been doing about this during these days, and especially for supporting my father's full rights and expressing concern for his current situation. I think I would ask the United States and everyone to continue to press China for his release and not to forget his case. I hope that all efforts can be continued. Thank you.*

I had made it through the first question. It didn't seem so bad to me. But then came the next one.

**Chairman Brown**: *What is your sense, Ms. Ilham, of the growing violence in Xinjiang?*

**Jewher**: *I'm sorry?*

**Chairman Brown**: *What is your sense of the growing violence in Xinjiang?*

Lawrence Liu, the staff director for the committee, had told me that I might be asked about issues in Xinjiang. But they asked it in a different way than how I prepared to answer. My answer couldn't work out. I had to change it. First, I was thinking, how should I organize my English? I'm going to screw up everything, just make it bad. I knew if I answered this one way, Uyghur people might get angry. But if I answered it another way, Chinese people would get angry. But then I also remembered Lawrence had said it was okay to say that I didn't know the answer to any questions about China and politics; that what I did know about was my father.

**Jewher**: *Well, I'm not an expert, an academic expert on Xinjiang, but I think I, my father, and most of the Uyghur people, I think nobody really wants violence and nobody wants to hurt innocent people. So some people, a few Uyghur people, now use violence but that doesn't mean that everybody wants to do like that. Also, it doesn't mean that my father supports this violence.*

**Chairman Brown**: *Okay. Okay.*

**Jewher**: *That's what he struggles for, to let people change their mind.*

**Chairman Brown**: *Okay. Thank you, Ms. Ilham.*

All of us were asked more questions. I took some about the effects of my father's arrest on our family, and about the charges. Sometimes I needed to look back to the translator—I wanted to make sure I was understanding the questions correctly, and I answered the best way I knew, explaining in some details the negative effects it especially was having on my brother and his schoolwork.

Toward the end, Representative Wenz asked all of us a very interesting question, but one I totally didn't know how to answer. He asked that since China is a very powerful country, how the U.S. confronts issues of human rights, such as with my father, might affect economic trade. He said, "Because it's going to come back to economic issues on that. That's going to make the leverage and that's going to hurt if we choose to do so."

What does that mean? I turned around. "Translator," I said. "Please translate!" It was so weird. I understood each single word. There was no difficult vocabulary. But when Representative Wenz asked the whole the question, I just didn't understand.

Even when it was translated into Chinese, I thought, how will I answer this? How should I know? I am not a business school student. And how should I know? *Why am I getting this kind of hard question?*

First Sophie Richardson answered. And then the Professor. And then Teng Biao.

Now it was my turn. *Why am I getting this kind of hard question?* Somebody please just help. I really didn't know how to answer. *Why am I getting this kind of hard question?*

I think when he looked at me, the congressman must have seen that my face was saying, *what?*

He just said, "My time is about up."

I said to myself, "Thanks, my God."

It finished shortly after that. Maybe only one hour in all, although it felt like ten hours, because I was so nervous.

Answering questions at the CECC Hearing

WHEN I STOOD UP, someone was grabbing my hair, touching my shoulders. I was shocked. Why would they do that? I just walked away. Straight back to the office again. To hide. I tried not to look back, not even turn my head. Later, Amy explained to me that there was one woman touching my hair, and another woman touching my shoulders. Both were trying talk with me. One it turned out was a reporter. Another was a Uyghur woman who I didn't know.

There were a few people were knocking on the office door that wanted to meet me, but I refused.

To tell you the truth, I was so hungry. I connected with a couple who I wanted to meet, but then I found Alexi and Jennifer. I wanted to eat. But then Alexi mentioned shopping. Could food wait? "Yes!!!" I said. Believe me, shopping was on mind, but I was afraid to suggest it. So when Alexi said that—Yes! I needed to explode! I'd just finished my midterm exam. The testimony.

I bought one dress; a flower one. I'd only brought sixty dollars with me to Washington. I'm a student; I don't have that much money. I spent seventeen dollars on clothes, twelve dollars on food, and twenty dollars for the shuttle from Bloomington to Indianapolis.

I got home with ten dollars in my pocket. That was good because I don't have much money. My mom was the only one who had been supporting me. From her salary—which is equal to about sixteen hundred US dollars—she sends me one thousand every month, and then lives on six hundred.

One thousand dollars is hard to live on. Rent. Busses. School supplies. Also every two months I have to pay two hundred and thirty dollars for my insurance – as an international. And I had to buy all the furniture, and all the home stuff.

So think about how much do I have left for food.

A lot of people are suspecting that I'm taking money from political organizations and from Uyghurs. But we, my family, are spending our own money.

From the beginning, we decided not to take any money from organizations tied to the Uyghur politics because we didn't want my father to fall into more trouble because of that. We were trying to let my father get rid the government's idea that he was having contact with overseas organizations. If I accepted money, that obviously meant that I had had contact with them. I only took money from universities like IU, and also PEN when the awarded my father the Freedom to Write award.

So yes, I bought one dress after the testimony. For seventeen dollars.

I BELIEVED MY TESTIMONY was going to be big for my father. That maybe it would even work to help his case. Or at least work to help my family. To help protect them.

I'm the oldest child in my family. I have a responsibility to protect my family, even though I was still only nineteen at the time of the hearing. It's kind of weird to think about, but I really do feel I'm responsible for this family and my stepmom. She's not weak woman; she just has no power.

I have no power too. But at least I am meeting people who have power and will try to let me let them help.

JEWHER BUSIES HERSELF IN *her apartment's kitchen,*
*preparing the meal. Sometimes she is talking with the refrigerator*
*door open; sometimes while on tiptoes, searching through the*
*cabinets. Sometimes she sings, her voice rising just above the sizzling*
*onions. Her father's trial is only a day and a half away (based on the*
*time difference). Tomorrow, with less than twenty-four hours before*
*it will start, we will be sitting with Elliot at a table in the Starbucks*
*on South Indiana Street (which Jewher affectionately refers to as*
*Elliot's office), across from the Sample Gates, the gateway to the Old*
*Crescent--the historic section of the Indiana University campus.*
*There, Elliot will have some pretrial updates from the lawyers,*
*translating them from Chinese into English. On occasion he will*
*stop, and in Chinese ask Jewher for help with a particular word,*
*careful to capture the precise nuance. In turn, he'll do the same*
*for her in English during conversation. The news he is translating*
*will not be encouraging. The sense is to hope for the best of a bad*
*situation. Yet within that hope, one senses a certain resignation—at*
*least for this stage. Afterward, Elliot and Jewher will compare lists*
*of interview requests—from the* Washington Post *to the* New York
Times *to blogs—with Elliot advising which ones Jewher should do.*
*But that all will come the following day. For now the focus is on*
*the cooking, and the joy of the meal. A celebration of being in the*
*present.*

**Jewher**: *We call it* dapanji. *In English: Big Plate Chicken. It is*
*another meal Uyghur people like to eat. Very popular in Xinjiang.*
*It is pieces of chicken cooked together with many spices and served*
*on a big platter.*

*The dapanji becomes a stew that also has potatoes, onions,*
*garlic, cumin, ginger, bell peppers, and . . .*

*Oh. Oh, no! Can we go to the Chinese grocery store now?*
*Obo's. It's just up the street on East 3rd. I still need to get the most*
*important ingredients – the noodles and more chilies.*

*But I am going to have to substitute* dao xiao mian *noodles for*
latiaozi *noodles. I shouldn't be using them because they actually*

*are for noodle soup. The* latiaozi *noodles that go with the* dapanji *are supposed to be wider and thicker. They usually are handmade, but already it is too late. I don't have time. It will take too long. So we will get* dao xiao mian—*the only wide noodles they have at the Chinese store.*

*And, just like with the pilaf I made for you the other night, the* dapanji *has to be very spicy. These red chilies will make it very spicy. And make it smell good.*

**Editors**: *I'll take you, but you at least have to let me pay for the chilies and the noodles, and whatever other ingredients you get at the store. You have to let me pay.*

**Jewher**: *No. You cannot pay. I will not accept. You are my guests. I am cooking for you in my house. And tonight you will eat even more. You won't be shy. Two plates. Three plates. Maybe more. It is my tradition. The tradition of Uyghur people.*

# PART SIX

In Washington, just after the testimony had finished, I met Sarah Hoffman for the first time. She was so kind, and at the time, she worked for PEN American Center in New York. She told me that PEN American Center had awarded my father the Barbara Goldsmith Freedom to Write Award for 2014.

Later I learned from Suzanne Nossel, the Executive Director at PEN, that they'd picked my father because his was a compelling case of someone unjustly accused, and they thought it might make a difference because he hadn't yet been tried or sentenced. It was explained to me that 34 of 37 winners over the years had been released from jail within an average of about 18 months from receiving the award. There also was a monetary award to help the family when the writer is in jail, or to help after the release. It was quite an honor.

I was a little surprised when they asked me to go to the gala to accept my father's award. I also was a little worried. Mostly because it was during my final exam time and I thought to myself, "Oh my god, here we go again! Another missed class, another speech I have to write!" I couldn't get rid of the nerves.

ON MAY 5, I went to the gala (absent from my class again). It was strange for me when I first arrived. The event was held at the American Museum of Natural History in New York City. Right near Central Park. There was a long cascade of steps leading up to the entrance, and a fancy blue light that lit up everything. It felt more like a castle than a museum. And inside, at the reception, were so many people. It was amazing. I think of myself as an unknown person, a non-famous girl. Meanwhile everyone else at the gala was very famous. Writers. Film directors. Celebrities. I felt like I was the only one that nobody knew.

Everyone was so dressed up. It was the fanciest thing I'd even be to. Beforehand, I'd been so nervous to find a dress that would be good enough. I'd shopped for two full days. Nothing was ever right. In the end, I settled for an old dress I had in the back of my closet. A short white dress that dropped right above my knees, with long, pretty white sleeves made of lace. Because May 5 also happened to be Doppa Cultural Day (a day which celebrates Uyghur culture), on my head I wore a doppa—a traditional Uyghur hat that is very colorful. And finally, I wore red 10-centimeter high heels. I had never worn heels in my life! It was so new for me.

I sat at a table at the front with Salman Rushdie, Pussy Riot, and Toni Morrison. A big whale was above us, hanging down from the ceiling. I had no idea who any of them were. Elliot was so excited when he found out we would be at the same table as them. I didn't know how regarded Salman Rushdie was, or that Toni Morrison was a Nobel Prize winner. So when Elliot told me all about them, and how famous and great they were, I got mad at him. "Why did you have to tell me this?" I said. "I thought at the very least I would comfortable sitting at my table. Now I am nervous!"

Now that I knew how special they were, I was worried I would sit wrong or eat wrong. Sometimes a camera would face the table, projecting me onto a big screen for everyone one to see. I had no idea what to do. On the table was this sign with #FreeIlham across it, and every time the camera came my way I picked it up and showed it. That was the only thing I could think to do.

After dinner came the awards. My speech followed Salman Rushdie. Suzanne Nossel went onto the stage to introduce my father and me. First, she played a video of my testimony. Oh my god, I was so embarrassed! All the eyes in the room were on my video. How embarrassed I was to see myself up there. After that, it showed footage of my father from before he got detained. I became suddenly very quiet. It had been such a long time since I had seen my father's face. Especially like this, moving. It felt like he was in front of me. My fingers started shaking so hard. My whole body started to shiver.

The video finished, and Suzanne asked me to come to the stage. I almost didn't hear her; I was still so nervous and flustered from seeing my father on the screen like that. Now I had to get up and walk up to the podium, with everyone looking at me going from my table. It was only then that I remembered my 10-centimeters heel. *Don't fall, Jewher. Don't fall.* Why of all places did I choose to wear heels here for the first time?

When I got up to the stage, I looked down. All I saw was darkness, except for the front seats. Sometimes when I mess up my English I make funny facial expressions. They are reflexes, and I don't really know how to stop them from happening. I thought: *Oh my god, they can see my face so clearly.* I was so worried I would do those faces up there on the stage, with everyone watching.

I concentrated on my facial expressions, and, just two months after I had testified in Washington, D.C., I gave my second speech to a room full of powerful strangers.

After I finished reading my remarks, I asked everyone to take a picture with the hashtag #FreeIlham, and then to post it on Facebook and Twitter. Social media seemed like the best way I could help my father—especially with so many celebrities being there. If they talked about my father, then more people would know about him. And from there, more people would get involved.

So while holding a #FreeIlham sign, I also had pictures taken with everyone I could: Salman Rushdie. Pussy Riot. All of them. Even my favorite writer, Malcolm Gladwell.

I was calmer at the gala than at the testimony. I think it was because of seeing the video of my father. It felt more like I was telling a story and less like I was trying to prove something. Both experiences meant so much to me, but they were so different. At the gala, I felt like everyone—even if they were strangers and celebrities—became my friends. At least, they were there for me as friends. Where as at the testimony, the tone was more serious. For the hearing, I was Ilham Tohti's daughter; I was regarded as his advocate. But at the gala, I was just his daughter. Just a nineteen-year-old girl.

**JEWHER'S ACCEPTANCE SPEECH** FOR the 2014 PEN/ Barbara Goldsmith Freedom to Write Award on behalf of her father, Ilham Tohti, at the PEN American Gala on May 5, 2014.

*Thank you very much for the honor that you are granting to my father this evening. Thank you too for giving me the opportunity to stand in his place and accept it.*

*Frankly, I had never imagined that I would in such a situation. I never thought that one day my father would be in imprisoned in Xinjiang, and I would be on the other side of the world trying my best to speak for him. This is not something I have ever prepared for, and I hope you will forgive my unpolished English, and my nervousness, which is increased by being in presence of so many renowned writers and activists.*

*My father, Ilham Tohti, has used only one weapon in his struggle for the basic rights of Uyghurs of Xinjiang: words. Spoken. Written. Distributed. And posted. This is all that he has ever had at his disposal, and all that he has ever needed. And this is what China finds so threatening.*

*Location may differ. Countries and societies may differ. But fear of free speech, and the power of words still sadly tortures the minds of so many of those who rule.*

*My father spoke up, and will continue to speak out for those who have been wrongly imprisoned, who have been beaten, who have been discriminated against because of their religion, language, and culture, and who have been disappeared. His work is not simply something for the Uyghurs. It is for China too. And for everyone in our common world society.*

*To have someone who has been imprisoned for his dream of a society founded on basic rights, and who is locked far away in a prison in the ancient Silk Road regions recognized this evening here in New York by PEN fills me with hope. To know that the person whom you honored is my father fills me with humility.*

*Thank you. Thank you very much.*

# PART SEVEN

My BIGGEST FEAR IS that my father will be forgotten. I do not want people to forget about him. So many bad things happen every day, and the media has to concentrate on the new stories. It makes me worried that my father will become old news, and, even though he is stuck in prison, people will forget about him because nothing new has happened to make him interesting again. Will his isolation make him forgettable?

Every time something big happens, I get this pit of worry in my stomach. Over the summer there was the World Cup, and I thought, oh my god, this is going to capture everybody's attention and they are going to forget about my father's case. Any time something like that happens—good or bad—I worry that my father will become less important.

My goal is to post as often as I can on social media. And right now, I am worried because there are no events going on. For a few months—with the testimony and the gala—I was so busy and there was a lot of attention on my father's case. But now things have slowed down. There have been no formal interviews or scheduled events.

For now, I am waiting for the trial. It is only a few days away. September 17, 2014. It is scary to think about. I know the news will pick back up again around that time, but still, that could be all for bad reasons.

With father and brother in Xinjiang (2011)

HERE IS SOME OF what I have learned:

**Time**

It tells you everything. Time tells you who to trust and how to trust.

But you have to be patient. You can't jump right into action; that might make it worse. Give the government time and maybe they will do the right thing. If you don't give them time to work that through, they will push back. They can always change their minds.

And remember to stay calm. Watch what you say. Whatever you say is going to influence your life and your family's life.

**Eyes**

They can reveal a lot about a person. They tell you whether a person is trustworthy. And if they are kind.

**Hobbies**

Focus on them—whatever they may be. For me, dance and drawing are my releases. They make me happier and more relaxed despite what has happened to my father. Dealing with this situation can be difficult, but finding a hobby to distract yourself, that is easy. And not only do they make you happy, but they can also improve your ability to...I don't know how to explain it well in English...but to *think* more. To understand more.

**Hope**

We have to remember, that no matter where we are there are always going to be good people. Whether I am there in China, or here in America, or in another country in between, there are going to be both good people and bad people. It doesn't matter the country or the religion or the ethnic group. Good people exist in the same places where bad people exist.

We can't just judge a whole group of people or a whole place based on the actions of a few.

We can't lose our hope. If I lose hope than I can never help my father. I wouldn't be able to do anything. I need to have trust. I need to let others in. If I don't, then I won't have anyone to help me. Then there would be nothing to do to help my father.

**Trust**

Trust is important.

**Editors**: DO YOU HAVE ANY REGRETS?

**Jewher**: Yes. One: that I didn't know how to cook when I was in China. My father really wanted me to cook for him. It was one of his biggest dreams, really. It sounds funny, I know, but in China, it's a very proud thing to eat your daughter's food. He wanted to see me become a real, independent adult. And now I am, but he can't see.

**Editors**: He will. He will see.

**Jewher**: I want him to see soon. Not after ten or fifteen years…

**Editors**: What is the first meal that you would make for him?

**Jewher**: Pilaf! And lahman. His favorite.

**Editors**: When was the last time you looked at the suitcase?

**Jewher**: My father's?

**Editors**: Yes.

**Jewher**: When Elliot was here. A few months ago. I took a shirt from it. The whole suitcase is huge, so I leave it at Elliot's. But sometimes I need something from it, to feel closer to my father. Sometimes I wear the shirt. At home. But on me, it is so big. It's like a dress.

**Editors**: Anything else you'd want to talk about that we haven't covered? We want to make sure we have everything.

**Jewher**: No, I think that is everything. For now.

OF COURSE I WOULD go back to China, if I could. If I could go back and be with my family I would. Definitely. It is where I am from. I grew up there. I can't just say I will never go back. It is impossible to give up on your home like that.

I still have a lot of mixed feelings about China. Even though the government did bad things to my family, I can't blame China. Like I mentioned before, wherever there are bad people, there are also many good people. That is true of every nationality: American, French, Mexican, Chinese, Turkish—whatever. Whoever you are, they are.

Even bad people, they aren't all bad. We can't label people that way. Are all the prisoners in jail bad people? No. They might have done bad things, but we can't just assume that they are totally bad people.

Like my father, he is in prison, but is he bad? No. But to some people, they think my father is a bad guy, and that is because they don't understand the whole truth.

So I can't say China is a bad place. It is my home. I like America better, but that doesn't mean America is full of good.

It all depends on how you look at things.

# POSTSCRIPT

IN THE MONTHS FOLLOWING *the interviews with Jewher (and at the time of this writing), the following key events took place:*

**September 23, 2014**
Following a two day, closed-door trial, the Intermediate People's Court of Urumqi convicted Ilham Tohti of separatism. The court said Professor Tohti had "bewitched and coerced young ethnic students" and through his website "encouraged his fellow Uyghurs to use violence." His assets and properties also were seized. The ruling was publicly condemned from the White House to the European Union.

**November 21, 2014**
Following an appeal by Professor Tohti's lawyers, the court upheld the separatism conviction and life sentence.

**December 9, 2014**
Seven of Ilham Tohti's students were convicted and jailed, accused of participating on Professor Tohti's website.

**January 16, 2015**
Nearly two years since Jewher Ilham and her father were detained and separated in the airport in Beijing, and one year since her

father was taken from his home, Jewher posts on social media: "I wanna go back to my childhood years, when my father would push me on the swing. But nowadays, I have no opportunities to relax and play. Now when I get on a swing I have to swing by myself."

# AFTERWORD
## ROBERT QUINN,
## EXECUTIVE DIRECTOR, SCHOLARS AT RISK NETWORK
## NEW YORK CITY

JEWHER ILHAM'S INSPIRING WORDS on behalf of her father, Ilham Tohti, a scholar imprisoned in China, resonate with a daughter's love and the anguish of a family, and a people, destroyed by callous authority. Jewher forces us once again to ask 'Why?' Why persecute this man, this family? Why is a powerful state still so afraid of simple ideas?

The answer lies in part in the man. What did Tohti do? He used the Internet to share his ideas about the rights and well-being of the Uyghur people. He did not call for violence. He did not call for the overthrow of a government. He exercised the right of freedom of expression, expressly protected by human rights treaties to which China is a signatory, and he suffered loss of his profession, surveillance, detention, prosecution and a sentence of life imprisonment. Of course he knew the risks; he was warned to be silent. But he spoke up anyway, committed to his people and to using nonviolent, legal means to seek justice for them.

The real answer comes from asking why China—why any state—comes down so hard on scholars like Tohti. Scholars do not hold military, political or economic power. Scholars operate in the realm of ideas, evidence and truth. Confident states might simply ignore them. But sensitive states whose authority rests on controlling information cannot, because scholars like Tohti stand at the intersection of power and ideas, of coercion and persuasion. Their willingness to suffer the consequences exposes the limits of coercive authority, which can be very threatening. So they attack scholars like Tohti to send a message to everyone that some areas of inquiry are off limits, some analysis is too dangerous, some opinions unspeakable.

That is why all of us have a stake in what happens to Jewher, Tohti, and the hundreds, perhaps thousands, of courageous women and men like them in China and around the world currently detained for their ideas. They all deserve our help. Thanks to Jewher, Tohti is not silenced. Through her courage and perseverance, Jewher reminds us that we all benefit from the sacrifices of Tohti and other scholars who are pushing the world past dependence on coercion toward reliance on evidence, reason and persuasion. Jewher reminds us that we campaign for Tohti because his vision, his future, is ours too.

You can help. Join Scholars at Risk's advocacy for Tohti and other scholars in prison. Urge your state to support greater protection for free inquiry and universities under attack. Urge your university to join the over 350 higher education institutions in Scholars at Risk's global network. And add your voice to those who won't be silenced by joining the *#free2think* campaign, pioneered by students at Roger Williams University on Tohti's behalf. Write down something you are grateful to be free to think about and snap a picture, using the *#free2think* hashtag. Then post it on Twitter, Facebook, or other sites to spread the word among your friends and colleagues asking them to join you and Scholars at Risk in fighting for Jewher, Tohti and for everyone's freedom to think, ask questions and share ideas, freely and safely.

*Scholars at Risk is an international network of higher education institutions and individuals working to protect persecuted scholars and promote academic freedom worldwide. To learn more, join the network or make a donation visit* www.scholarsatrisk.org.

*Photo: Echo Lu*

**Ashley Barton** worked as a member of the Advocacy Seminars as an undergraduate at Roger Williams University. Her advocacy work, particularly on the Ilham Tohti case, led to her being honored as a 2015 Newman Civic Fellow, a national award recognizing student leaders from undergraduate programs who create lasting change in their local and international communities. Ashley is currently in her first year of law school at Wake Forest University School of Law in Winston-Salem, North Carolina.

**Adam Braver** is the author of five novels, most recently *Misfit*. His books have been translated into several languages worldwide. Braver's short works and essays have appeared in numerous magazines. He is writer-in-residence at Roger Williams University, and also teaches at the NY State Summer Writers Institute.